300+
Sizzling
Icebreakers

300+ Sizzling Icebreakers

For cell churches, home groups & youth work

Michael Puffett
and
Blair Mundell

MONARCH
BOOKS

Oxford, UK and Grand Rapids, Michigan, USA

First published in the UK in 2009 by Monarch Books
(a publishing imprint of Lion Hudson plc),
Wilkinson House, Jordan Hill Road, Oxford OX2 8DR.
Tel: +44 (0)1865 302750 Fax: +44 (0)1865 302757
Email: monarch@lionhudson.com
www.lionhudson.com

ISBN 978-1-85424-919-7 (UK)
ISBN 978-0-8254-6318-1 (USA)

Distributed by:
UK: Marston Book Services Ltd, PO Box 269,
Abingdon, Oxon OX14 4YN;
USA: Kregel Publications, PO Box 2607
Grand Rapids, Michigan 49501.

This book has been printed on paper and board independently certified as having come from sustainable forests.

British Library Cataloguing Data
A catalogue record for this book is available
from the British Library.

Printed and bound in Malta by Gutenberg Press.

Dedication

To Jubilee Church, our precious family in Christ.
This book is dedicated to you.

We trust that the life in these pages is an accurate representation
of what you have fostered over the years.

Thank you, Jubilee, for your continual commitment to our vision.

Contents

Nowhere to Hide 41

Energizers 57

Getting the Word In   74

Open-Heart Surgery   89

Pandora's Box 97

Q & A 102

Events for the Masses   110

Ready-made Small Group Nights   115

Teamwork 146

Acknowledgments

A huge thank you to all who helped with this project. Sylvie Mundell, Paul and Justine Houghton, Tim and Sinta Price, Chris and Shae Williams, Nicky Kendall, Suzanne Darling, Suzi Steele, Diedre Campbell, John and Canja Cable, John Baxter, Dan Maudhub, Taryn Terlecki, Laura Finn and Ralf Helfrich. You guys are the best!

Foreword

Another book of icebreakers you cry; why do we need this? Icebreakers are growing in popularity in the context of small groups and are used in almost any gathering of people – the question I am often asked is, 'Why?' It is because there are three things that icebreakers do in an amazing way:

1. *They give everybody a voice.* Often our models of church put higher value on the voice of our leaders and the voice of the people can be lost. An icebreaker – particularly in a small group or a cell – tells us that a meeting is about participation and that everybody has something to contribute.

2. *They encourage honesty and sharing.* When someone contributes through an icebreaker something important happens: they see that they are treated with respect, and it is this that helps to build trust within the group. As a result, they may feel able to share something more personal in future gatherings.

3. *They build community.* As we share our stories and contributions we slowly learn more about each other and as we do so we become more important to each other. Our emotions are engaged and the people within the group become more and more real to us. What began with a group of strangers has become a group of friends – you are part of a community.

I highly recommend *300+ Sizzling Icebreakers* – it will give people a voice, it will encourage honesty and it will build community.

Laurence Singlehurst
Director of Cell UK

Foreword

It is a privilege to write this foreword for my friend Michael. I first became acquainted with him when he spoke at our annual youth conference in September 2008. I knew instantly that we had found a friend for life.

Michael is a true father in the Lord and a brother in Christ who walks the talk. The reach of his ministry has gone far beyond his native South Africa and England, where he now lives, to the nations where he is having a remarkable influence across the generations.

The book you now hold in your hand is a valuable resource for facilitators of groups of all sizes. The ideas are fun, easy to follow, and require very few props – all you need is a little imagination and your group will come alive.

Revd Josephine Kok
Generation Church, Toronto

Breaking People in Slowly

'Community is the window through which people see Jesus.'
Michael Puffett

We are called to be people who foster community. In this context, icebreakers are an effective tool to bring people together. They are non-threatening, allow the group to interact, and place people gently outside of their comfort zone. Icebreakers not only help to build community, they also bring a much-needed injection of energy and life. Never underestimate just how predictable and boring we can make our small groups, meetings and celebrations. Although we plan to make them fun, the people we lead become comfortable in their habits very quickly. To help to overcome this, here are a few icebreakers.

10 Tips for Breaking People in Slowly

1   If you fail to prepare, you prepare to fail.

2   Keep the members of your small group guessing – use the element of surprise. This keeps people excited and on their toes.

3   Keep the atmosphere informal; don't announce what you are about to do next in a formal manner, for example: 'And now for the icebreaker.'

4   To start off the icebreaker, pick people who will really go for it, as a more embarrassed person will set the tone for the rest. If need be, be prepared to start yourself!

5   Keep fun icebreakers simple.

6   Do not get too competitive or you will lose the fun side of it.

7   Prepare all of your props to avoid wasting time during the meeting.

8   Make sure everyone participates, especially visitors who may be feeling left out or uncomfortable.

9   If you are leading the show, you should be having the most fun: As the leader, you will set the vibe and establish the tone for the rest of the meeting.

10   Keep the prizes simple and cheap. Don't hesitate to use creativity!

Triple Threat

You will need:

✳ **Paper and pens**

Each person should write down three intriguing questions on a piece of paper, such as 'What was the toughest work situation you have ever been in?' or 'What is your dream holiday destination?' Then get everyone to mingle and ask each other the questions on their piece of paper. Go around the group and ask each person what the most interesting questions and answers that they came across were.

What's that Whiff?

Ask each person to describe their favourite smell, and to explain what makes it their favourite smell.

'Who's in da House?'

You will need:

✳ **Paper and pens**
✳ **Bowl or hat**

Each person in the group must choose a name for themselves. It can be the name of a real person, dead or alive, or a fictional character. Once they have chosen a name, they must write it on a piece of paper and place it in a bowl/hat without telling anyone else what they have chosen. When everyone has handed in their paper, get someone to read out all of the names to the group.

The object of the game is to guess who chose which name. Get one person to guess at a time. If they guess correctly the first time round, that person can form a group with the one whose character it was, and becomes the leader of that group. The guessing should continue until there is one individual who is un-guessed and a group whose leader is un-guessed. The person who has the correct last guess, and thus remains un-guessed, wins!

Lights, Camera, Action!

Ask each member to act out their day in thirty seconds.

Blind Man's Art

You will need:

✳ **Blindfold**

✳ **A box with random items and objects**

✳ **Pencils and pens**

✳ **Paper**

Get two people to sit back to back, one of them blindfolded with a collection of objects set before them. The other person is the 'artist' and needs a pen and paper. The blindfolded person must choose a random object from the collection and try to describe it to the 'artist'. The 'artist' must then attempt to draw what has been described. The blindfolded person is not allowed to name the object; they must simply describe it. Once the artwork is finished they can look to see how accurate the drawing is! To make the icebreaker more fun you can time it and have various pairs competing at the same time. The pairs can also then swap roles.

What Floats Your Boat?

You will need:

✳ **One small blow-up plastic swimming pool**

✳ **An 'activity pack' for each person taking part, consisting of paper, matchsticks, glue or sticky tape.**

Blow up the swimming pool and place it on a waterproof plastic sheet in the middle of the floor. Give each person their 'activity pack'. They will have ten minutes to make a boat (or a sturdy floatable object). Once completed, the boats/floatable objects can be placed all around the pool. On the word 'Go!', each person must blow their boat across to the other side of the pool. The first person to cross wins. The funny part of this icebreaker is that when the boats reach the middle of the pool, it becomes total chaos and guarantees a belly laugh!

Picasso Portraits

You will need:

∗ **Paper and pencils**

Get everyone to sit in a circle. Give each person a piece of paper and a pencil and ask them to draw a profile portrait of the person sitting on their right-hand side. Allocate five to seven minutes to finish before collecting all the pictures. Show the portraits to the group and allow them to guess who is in each picture.

Did You Know?

You will need:

∗ **A number of questions on individual pieces of paper, such as:**

- **What is your fondest childhood memory?**
- **When it comes to holidays, are you more of a beach bum or an action hero?**
- **What is the naughtiest thing you have ever done?**

∗ **Container**

Fold the questions and put them into an open container. Give each person a chance to pick a question out of the container, read it aloud, and give their answer to the group.

Greedy Game

You will need:

∗ **A roll of toilet paper**

Pass the roll of toilet paper around the group and ask each person to take as much as they would need if they were stuck on a desert island for a week. This may mean that some people take plenty and others have nothing. Once everyone has taken their share, instruct the group to tell everybody something about themselves for every block of paper they have taken. Get each person to share one at a time.

Breakdown

Call out various categories such as favourite food or sport, hair colour or month of birth. As you call out a category, the group must find people who fall into the same category as themselves. By doing this, the group will subdivide itself into smaller groups and people will see what they have in common with each other. Try at least ten categories so that they all interact!

For another version of this game, run it in complete silence. It is amazing what people will come up with to communicate with one another!

Sit/Stand/Lie Down

You will need:

* **A chair**

Ask people to get into groups of three. Give each group a scenario such as a 'bank scene' or 'life in a dental surgery'. Each person in the group should be given, or choose, a character, and the group must act out the scene as a drama in front of the rest of the people. At any one time, one person must be standing, one sitting, and the other lying down. Throughout the scene, the individuals will have to change positions, but none of them must be allowed to be in the same position: so, if one is standing, the others need to sit or lie down. The group must be continually watchful of each other in order to quickly change positions, whilst still acting out their drama.

Chaos Communication

Get the group to arrange themselves in a line by date of birth, year of birth, age, weight and so on. They may not speak to each other or use pen and paper, but must communicate by means of sign language or drama.

Mount Shoe

Get everybody to remove one of their shoes and place it in the centre of the room. Once everyone has removed a shoe, invite people to each take one shoe from the pile in the centre. The object of this icebreaker is to find the person whose shoe you have and the person who has your shoe. Upon meeting them, introduce yourself and get to know them.

ID Analysis

You will need:

＊ **Pens**

＊ **Paper**

Get everyone to write three statements about themselves on a piece of paper. For example: What food they like, their job and where they were born. Hand out the pieces of paper randomly. The object is to find the person whose paper you have, and to find the person who has your paper. Upon meeting them, introduce yourself and get to know them.

Got Your Back!

You will need:

＊ **One A4 piece of paper and a pen per person taking part**

＊ **Sticky tape**

Stick a piece of paper on to each person's back. Get everyone in the room to write something that they like or admire about that person without putting their name on it. Once everyone has had a chance to write something down, put all the pieces of paper into a pile and ask someone to read each one out. The group must guess whose paper is being read. This icebreaker is a lovely way to encourage one another!

The Interview

✻ **3 silly hats**

Divide the group of people into teams of three people each. One person should take on the character of the interviewer, the other of the interviewee, and the third that of the cameraman. Make sure that each person is wearing a silly hat. The team must decide on a theme that becomes the reason the interview is taking place. They must then act out the scene to the best of their ability, one group at a time with the others watching. After a minute or so, somebody in the audience should shout 'Freeze!' The group then freezes. The person in the audience should get up, walk over to the group, swap their hats around and sit down, shouting 'Unfreeze!' The group must continue to act out the scene, but taking on the character that relates to the new hat they are wearing. After a minute or so, somebody else in the audience can shout 'Freeze' and so on, until everybody in the team has had a chance to play each character.

Picture This...

✻ **Pens and paper for each person taking part**

Each person can be given a pen and paper and asked to draw their day. When they have finished, give them one minute to describe it. However, before they go ahead, the group must guess what the picture is saying. This is a great icebreaker for people who find it naturally hard to talk about themselves.

If I Was...

Ask people to think about a car or an animal that has characteristics similar to their own. Go around the group and encourage people to share and to explain these similarities. This icebreaker helps people to get to know each other better.

Coin Chronology

Take a coin out of your purse or wallet. Tell the group what happened in your life in the year the coin was made. If the coin was made before you were born, choose another one.

Standing in Line

You will need:

* 10 good questions that will get people chatting.
For example:

- 'What do you think of the town you live in?'
- 'Where were you born?'
- 'What's your favourite TV show?'

* Music

Divide the group in half and arrange people into two straight lines facing each other. Play music in the background. When the music starts, get people to answer the first question. When the music stops, get the person standing at the end of one of the lines to move to the beginning of the line, giving each individual a new partner. Continue with the music and questions until all have been answered.

Christmas Jingle

You will need:

* A prize for the winning team

Break the group up into three teams. Each team must write a Christmas jingle to the tune of a well-known Christmas song. It can be on any Christmas-related topics such as presents, food, family times, even Jesus! Award a prize for the best jingle.

Playdough Charades/ Pictionary Charades

You will need:

✳ **A good quantity of playdough**

✳ **A list of random objects such as movies/TV programmes, famous shop names, locations, people, objects and so on. For example:**

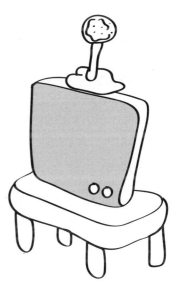

- *Titanic*
- *A Clockwork Orange*
- **Rio de Janeiro**
- **Danger Mouse**
- *Coronation Street*
- **Stade de France**
- **Johnny Clegg**
- **Genesis**
- **Batman**
- **Boots the Chemist**
- *Top Gear*
- **Eucalyptus**
- **Dr Who**

Break the group up into smaller teams. Have your list of items ready and get each team to simultaneously send a representative to you. Quietly read the first item on the list to all representatives and send them back to their teams. They will have to silently build this item using the playdough in order to get their team to guess it (or construct something which will help the team to guess what it is – for example, for *Top Gear*, build a car and a TV screen). Once it is guessed, the next person from that team should come up, give the answer to you to check and, if correct, can be read the next item on the list. This can continue until a team guesses all the items on your list.

For another version of this icebreaker, replace the playdough with A4 sheets of paper and pens. It then becomes a Pictionary Charade!

Blind Man's Buff

You will need:

✳ **Blindfold**

Get your group to play hide and seek in the house, following the usual rules of the game: Blindfold somebody and switch all the lights off. Send the others to pick a spot to hide. Tell them that once they have found their spot, they are not allowed to move. The blindfolded person must try to catch somebody. The next person to be blindfolded is the one who was caught!

'My Last Month' Poem

You will need:

✳ **Paper and pens**

Get the people in your group to write a short, ten-line poem about their last month. Encourage them to use plenty of humour and rhymes, whilst remaining detailed and realistic about what they got up to. It will surprise you to see how excited your people will be about writing this piece, and to hear the results.

The 'New Small Group Member' Welcoming Quiz

Have a quiz ready for each new person that attends/visits your small group. It is a great way to welcome them and make them feel special. Whether you choose to write a multiple choice questionnaire about the person or put together a series of standard and fun questions, this icebreaker will be a great way for people to start to get to know a little bit about the guest(s).

Examples of simple but fun questions:

● Who are you: Name, height, favourite colour?

● Where are you from?

● Any brothers and/or sisters?

● What's your day-to-day job?

● What is your earliest holiday memory and where was it?

- Which sport(s) or hobbies do you enjoy?
- Greatest achievement?
- What's your dream holiday destination?
- Favourite movie?
- Night owl or early bird?
- If you were an animal, what would you be and why?
- Sum up your past seven days in three words.

40-Inch Dash

You will need:
* **String**
* **Marshmallows**

This game is played with a few people in front of an audience. Give three volunteers a 40-inch piece of string with a marshmallow tied to one end of it. On a signal, each person must put the loose end of the string in their mouth and 'eat' their way to the marshmallow. The first person to reach it is the winner.

Alphabet Pockets

Divide into teams of four or five and get each person on the team to search through their own pockets, wallets, handbags and so on. Each group must try to come up with one possession which begins with each letter of the alphabet, for example: C – credit card, D – driving licence, P – photograph. The winning team is the one to have objects representing the most letters.

Atlas Small Group

Either in order of seating, or in a circle, the first person must say the name of any city, river, ocean or mountain that could be found on an atlas. The next person must say another place that starts with the last letter of the previous place. Set a ten-second limit and ensure that no place is repeated. Examples: Kenya, Athens, Seine, Estonia, Alps.

Balloon Catch

You will need:

∗ **Balloons**

∗ **Butterfly net, baseball glove or container**

Get three to four people to blow up large balloons without tying them. Have them attempt to 'throw' them across the room to a catcher holding a butterfly net, baseball glove, container, or something similar. The catcher must try to catch at least two out of five balloons in forty-five seconds. This icebreaker can be done in teams or as individuals. You may need to test this to determine what a decent catching distance would be.

Balloon Nose Pop

You will need:

∗ **A number of large balloons**

This game is played with a few people in front of an audience. Take large balloons and ask for three volunteers. Each person should receive a balloon. Tell them they must blow it up – using their nose. The first to blow up their balloon so far that the balloon pops, wins.

Banana Dress-Up

You will need:

∗ **A banana per team**

∗ **A bag of random items per group. It can contain things like felt material, foil, beads and so on. Be creative!**

Break the group up into smaller teams and give each team a banana and their bag of random items. Give the teams a few minutes to create a personality and appearance for their banana with the items they are given. At the end of the allocated time, a volunteer can introduce their banana to the whole group. It is better if each group is given different items to keep it varied.

Banana Poke

You will need:

* 2 bananas
* Some string

This game is played with a few people in front of an audience. Pick two volunteers to come upfront. Tie their left hands together and give them each a banana. The volunteers must peel the banana with one hand and try to poke the other person in the face with their banana. Watch out for one another's eyes!

Banana Surgery

You will need:

* A banana per team
* Some drawing pins, needles and thread, safety pins, sticky tape, glue
* A video feed to a big screen (optional)

Divide your group into teams. Without explaining why, get a team to peel and cut up a banana into equal parts. Then instruct them to put the banana back together using the drawing pins, needles and thread, safety pins, sticky tape or glue. The team with the best reconstructed banana wins.

If you do this with a big group, use a video feed to a big screen and time the surgery so it doesn't drag.

Most Favourite Gift

Ask one of the following questions and discuss as a group:

● What is the best gift that you have ever received?
● What gift would you most like to receive?

When I Go to Russia...

Get the group to sit in a circle. Start the game by saying, 'When I go to Russia I wear...' (Insert an item of clothing such as a coat). Subtly cross your arms as you speak – this becomes the secret rule that needs to be implemented by anybody who gets a chance to speak. Choose the next person to do the same, but after they have spoken you must tell them whether or not people wear what they chose in Russia. This is based on whether or not they have picked up on the secret rule! Repeat this around the circle, each time either agreeing or disagreeing with the person's fashion statement. The likelihood is that people in the group will get very frustrated trying to find the secret rule that determines what they can and cannot wear. It is extremely amusing for everyone who has worked out the rule. Play the game until everyone has caught on.

Who Am I?

You will need:

* **Pieces of paper**
* **Sticky tape**
* **Pens**

Write the name of a famous character on pieces of paper, and stick on the back of each person. People should ask each other questions which can be answered 'yes' or 'no' to find out who they are. For example: 'Am I in entertainment?' or 'Am I in sports?' Get them to keep going around asking different people questions until they can guess who they are.

Who in the Bible Am I?

As above, but the names on people's backs must be Bible characters.

What Am I?

Same as above but people will be, for example, an animal or object.

Find Your Partner

Same as above but get people to ask questions in order to find their partner, such as salt and pepper, or Samson and Delilah.

What a Surprise!

You will need:

* **Pieces of paper**

* **Sticky tape**

* **Pens**

* **Hat or container**

Get people to write down on a piece of paper an interesting fact about themselves that others do not know. Put all the pieces of paper in a hat or container and pick and read out one at a time. Get everyone to go around the room asking questions to find out who is matched with the fact. Once the group has established whose fact it is, pick another fact and so on.

Party Trick

Everyone has a party trick, something that gets the party going. Get each person to perform their party trick in front of the group.

The Chocolate Test

You will need:

* **Seven types of chocolate**

Get about seven different types of chocolate and divide the group into seven smaller teams. Break the chocolates into small pieces and ask teams to taste each type of chocolate in succession, writing down the brand of chocolate they just tasted. Make sure the teams are very specific. All teams will taste the same chocolate at the same time and move on to the next chocolate together. Be sure that you know which chocolate is which as the wrapper will have gone. Give one point per correct answer. The team with the most points wins.

Favourite Song

You will need:

* A CD player

Each person should bring a CD with their favourite song. After playing the song, get them to explain why it is their favourite. It could be, for example, their favourite love song, praise song, worship song, song that reminds them of healing, of hurting, or of fun moments.

String Intros!

You will need:

* Some string
* A pair of scissors

Take several pieces of string, cut them to various lengths and get everyone to take a piece. They must introduce themselves to everyone else, and as they speak they must wind the string around their finger until the string is finished. Obviously some will speak for much longer than others!

Bun Icing

You will need:

* Fairy cakes
* Coloured icing (make sure you have several colours available)
* Sweets, such as Smarties or Skittles

Give people an undecorated fairy cake and various tubes of coloured icing. Also supply the sweets that will be used as decorations. Ask people to decorate their cake according to what God is doing in their life at the moment, or how their week or day has been.

Cake Cutting

You will need:

* Flour in a bowl
* A little water
* A plate
* A kitchen knife
* A sweet
* Cloth or plastic sheeting

Make a cake from compacted flour in a bowl. Turn the cake out onto a plate and place a sweet on the top. Take turns cutting away the flour until someone makes the sweet fall from the top. Whoever makes the sweet fall can then have a forfeit. Be careful as this icebreaker can be a bit messy. Place a cloth or some plastic sheeting under the plate of flour.

Which Animal?

You will need:

* Playdough or putty

Distribute the playdough or putty to everyone in the group. Ask them to mould the animal which they think they are most like, and tell everyone why.

Mixed People

You will need:

✽ **A3 pieces of paper cut down the middle to create two long pieces with small widths**

✽ **Pens**

Divide the lengths of paper into five sections, and hand out a length to each person. Give everyone a pen and get them to draw a head in the top section of the length of paper with a little bit of the neck going slightly into the next section. Fold over the top section so the head that has just been drawn cannot be seen. However, make sure that two lines of the neck can be seen. Swap the pictures around in the group and follow the same process, each time drawing a different part of the body on the section of paper: upper body in the second section, elbow to wrist in the third, waist to knee in the fourth and knee to feet in the fifth. At the end, unfold the paper and discover the 'person' that has been created!

Alphabet Game

You will need:

✽ **A4 sheets of paper**

✽ **Pens**

Give everyone a piece of paper and a pen and get them to divide their page into five columns, heading them up as follows: boy's name, girl's name, animal, country, thing. Select one person to start saying the alphabet in their head, starting at any point and repeating it through until you say 'Stop!' The person should then call out the letter that they stopped on and each person is given twenty seconds to fill out the columns with a word for each category, beginning with that letter. For example, for the letter 'A', someone might write 'Adam/Andrea/Anteater/Angola/Aircraft'. The first person to complete all of the columns should yell 'Stop!' Answers must be compared and scores written down. Ten points can be awarded for answers that nobody else has, and five points if someone else has the answer. The game should be repeated, and at the end all of the scores can be added up. The aim of the game is to score the most points!

Beaky

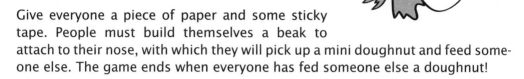

✳ **A4 sheets of paper**

✳ **Sticky tape**

✳ **A plate of mini doughnuts**

Give everyone a piece of paper and some sticky tape. People must build themselves a beak to attach to their nose, with which they will pick up a mini doughnut and feed someone else. The game ends when everyone has fed someone else a doughnut!

Lucky Dip

✳ **A whole lot of questions on single pieces of paper. For example:**

- ● **What countries have you travelled to?**
- ● **When was your last holiday, and what did you do?**
- ● **Who was your favourite teacher at school and why?**
- ● **Where did you get your first car from?**
- ● **What was your first job?**
- ● **What is the best gift you have ever received?**
- ● **What did you eat today?**
- ● **What is/was your favourite pair of shoes?**
- ● **Do you have/want any pets?**
- ● **Name one thing you would like to do before you die.**

✳ **Bowl or container**

Depending on the size of the group, aim to have at least three questions per person. Fold the paper and put it in a bowl or container. Pass the bowl/container around the group and take it in turns to pull out a piece of paper, read the question aloud, and answer it.

Spot the Difference

Ask everyone to team up with somebody that they don't know, or don't know very well. Each pair should face each other for five seconds. They must then turn back-to-back and change three things about their appearance (for example, take out an earring, unzip their jumper or untie a shoelace). They must then turn around and each guess which three things have been changed about the other person's appearance.

Airport

Each person in the group must have an opportunity to answer the following question:

● If you could live anywhere in the world, where would it be and why?

Making New Friends (1)

Divide the group into teams of four or five people. Team members have to find ten things they have in common with every other person in their team. These cannot be body parts or clothing. Get one person in the team to take note of what is said and to be ready to feedback from the list to the other teams.

Making New Friends (2)

You will need:

* Pens
* Sticky labels

Get people to write two adjectives that describe themselves onto a sticky label and stick it onto themselves. Each person must then find somebody else with similar or opposite adjectives and spend a couple of minutes discussing why they described themselves that way.

Paper Charades

You will need:

* List of items (such as kettle, dog, frog, tree, parrot, computer and so on)
* Old magazines, catalogues or newspapers

Divide the group into two or more teams made up of approximately four people. Have a list of items or names ready and get each team to simultaneously send a representative to you. Quietly read the first item on the list to all the representatives and send them back to their teams. Each team must be given an old magazine, catalogue or newspaper, so that the representative can tear it into the shape of the item. The other team members must then guess what the object is. No actions, gestures, noises or spelling should be allowed. The representatives must rely on their skill in tearing the paper in such a way that their team will be able to guess the object correctly. Once it is guessed, the next person from that team should come up, give the guess to you, and if correct can be read the next item on the list. This can continue until a team guesses all the items on your list.

You've Been Pegged!

You will need:

* 100 pegs

The challenge for each person is to try and fit as many pegs into one hand as they can without the pegs being attached to each other. The person able to hold the most is the winner.

Sausage

Get one person to sit in the middle of the group. Each person in the group should ask the one in the middle a question. The person in the middle must reply 'sausage' to every question. The aim of the game is to get this person laughing. Whoever succeeds in doing so must then sit in the middle and the process can be repeated.

Why I Am

Get each person to choose a musical instrument that they can compare themselves to. They can then explain the similarity between their personality and their chosen instrument.

Mosaic Story

You will need:

✳ **A set of sequential pictures**

The aim of this icebreaker is to create, as a group, a unified story from a set of sequential pictures. The pictures must be randomly ordered and handed out. Each person should have a picture, but cannot show it to others. One by one the pictures can be turned around and that part of the story is made up. This icebreaker requires patience, communication, and trying to understand another person's point of view in order to recreate the story sequence.

Nowhere to Hide

'Some people don't need to get out of their comfort zone;
they need to be thrown out of it!'
Blair Mundell

If you are looking for something a little more 'in your face', this section of the book is for you. From gross to ghastly, you will find it here! The youth, especially, will love this type of icebreaker. They are extreme, fun, and not for the faint-hearted!

6 Tips for Extreme Icebreakers

1 If you fail to prepare, you prepare to fail.

2 Make sure that you are prepared to do the icebreaker before expecting someone else to do it!

3 The more excited you are about it, the more excited others will be.

4 Do not pick on the same people over and over again.

5 If it is going to be messy, use plastic sheeting to protect the floor, tables and so on.

6 Make sure you clean up after yourself, especially if you are at someone else's home.

Ready Steady Advertise!

Here the members must be divided into groups of at least three, depending upon numbers. They can each be given a random object and then given ten minutes to come up with a thirty-second advert for it – which they should then act out to the group.

Whose Line is it Anyway?

You will need:

✳ A box filled with all kinds of props, such as random clothing and objects

A designated person should begin by picking up an object and then acting something ad-lib with it. The second person should get up and join their 'story' with another object. A third person must then join the 'story', which is the cue for the first person to leave. However, they must leave by tying up their 'end' of the 'story' and leaving their object back in the box; they may not just walk off stage. By the end of the 'drama', each person should have had a chance to act. Actors can come up 'on stage' whenever they want and they don't necessarily have to only 'act' once.

Thinking Out of the Box!

You will need:

✳ 1 empty cereal box
✳ A pair of scissors

Give each person a chance to try to pick up an empty cereal box with their teeth. Tell them they are not allowed to use their hands, may bend in any position and may not put their knees on the floor. After each person has had a chance, you, the group leader, must cut a small section off (this is at your discretion). By the end of the game you should have the final challenge: a small, flat piece of cardboard on the floor. Whoever can pick this up successfully with their teeth is, of course, the winner – great for anyone who is a bit squeamish at getting out of their comfort zone!

A Tight Fit!

You will need:

* New, clean, cheap stockings/
tights

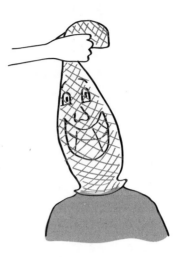

Each person should be given a piece of tights/
stockings to pull over their face. They should
then be slowly pulled up and, if done correctly,
the tights/stockings should distort their face into
some pretty hilarious expressions – great for getting those who are shy out of their shell!

Fashion Show

You will need:

* Music

Play the most outrageous music you can find! Arrange the room to look like a
fashion runway. Break the group into teams and get them to model the clothing they are wearing. Set up a panel of judges to critique each team. The more
extravagant the modelling, the more points the team receives.

Banana Tights

You will need:

* A pair of new, clean tights (20/40 denier) per four
people

Each player is handed a banana and half a leg from the tights (for the piece
without a foot, one end to be tied in a knot). Each person should put the tights
over their heads (like a balaclava) so that the whole face is covered right down
to the neck. The aim is for every player to begin eating the banana through the
tights at the same time, and the winner is the one who eats the whole banana
quickest. It can be done!

Battered Sweets

You will need:

* Jelly sweets (big and small)
* Water
* Flour
* Bowls
* Blindfolds

Two bowls should be half-filled with water and jelly sweets placed in the bottom of the bowls. Another two bowls can be filled with flour. Divide the group evenly and line up in relay style. At the end of the room have a bowl of flour and one of water and sweets for each team involved. Each team member must run to the other side of the room, and when they arrive at the bowls they should be blindfolded. The player must dunk their head into the water, fish a sweet out and place it at the bottom of the flour bowl. Then they must remove the blindfold and run back to the team and send the next person. The first team to finish fishing and battering all of the sweets is the winner. Be warned, there is plenty of mess!

Mummy Bake

You will need:

* Cling film
* 1 fairy cake per team
* Plates

Divide the group into two teams. Each team should have a roll of cling film and a fairy cake on a plate in the distance. The aim of the game is for each team to nominate a team member to be the mummy. Then the remaining team players will embalm the mummy with the whole roll of cling film (the mummy's hands must be by their sides in the cling film – no arms to be out of the cling film). Once the player is embalmed (without covering the face), they must make their way to the cake on the plate and eat it as quickly as possible with no assistance from their team members. The first mummy standing straight after embalming and eating is the winner.

Nose Spread

You will need:

∗ Toast

∗ Butter

∗ Spread of choice

The aim of the game is for two people to butter and spread a piece of toast. The first person butters and the second spreads – but the catch is that it is to be done using... their noses! You can add a third person for the gross factor who will have to eat the toast.

Baby Bottle Burp

You will need:

∗ 3 large towels

∗ 3 500 ml empty water bottles half filled with soda

Get three ladies put a nappy (towel) around three gentlemen, sit them on their lap, feed them a half full 'baby bottle' of soda, and make them burp. The first guy to burp wins!

Banana Barf

You will need:

∗ A banana per volunteer

∗ A pair of tights per volunteer (new and clean)

∗ Rubbish bin or plastic bag

This game is played with a few people in front of an audience. Have two or three volunteers put a whole banana in their mouth, instructing them not to eat it but to just hold it in their mouth. Then put a pair of tights over each volunteer's head. Have them squish the banana through the tiny holes in the tights into a rubbish bin or plastic bag.

Most Embarrassing Moment

Ask everyone in the group to share their most embarrassing moment.

Blindfold Feeding Game

You will need:

* A blindfold per pair
* A banana per pair

Put people into pairs and blindfold them. They have to feed each other something such as a banana.

What Do You Have?

You will need:

* Pens
* Paper

Divide the group into teams. Each team should make a list of six to eight items that they would probably have with them. Make one or two items less common things. The team will be awarded points for each person who has these items. Only one of each item can be counted per person, and the team with the most points wins. The list could include: a photograph, a calculator, a pencil, an unusual key ring.

Would You Rather...

This icebreaker is ideal for a small group setting. Ask your group a series of questions such as:

● Would you rather live your dream but have no money, or be in a job that pays you well but isn't really your passion?

● Marry a cruel billionaire, or a kind poor person?

● Be able to fly, or be able to read people's thoughts?

● Be able to sing well but be unknown, or sing badly and be famous?

You can think of your own questions to generate discussion about what's important in life.

SingStar® or Dance Mat

Set up SingStar or a dance mat for an evening of embarrassment. This requires a games console, for example Sony PlayStation.

Endurance with Mints

You will need:

✳ **A mint per person**

Get people to place one mint in their mouth. The one who holds it longest without spitting it out wins.

Bum Spelling

Spell out words in the air with your bum! The longer the word the better.

Doughnut Line

You will need:

✳ **Some string**

✳ **Mini doughnuts (or big doughnuts if you're daring enough!)**

Thread several doughnuts onto the string. Get two people to hold either side of the string, and as many others as possible to eat the doughnuts without using their hands. The catch is that the players holding the string must make it bounce and swing to make it difficult to eat.

H^{2}O Tunes

This icebreaker consists of gargling with water whilst singing a famous tune. These can be anything from worship songs to national anthems. Great fun! Break the group into teams and ask for volunteers to take the challenge. The rest of the team has to guess the tune. It is even more fun when done against the clock! Make sure you have a tea towel ready for the dribblers.

Scripture Revision

Pick a lengthy portion of scripture from the Bible and split the group into teams. Get each team to present the portion of scripture in various musical styles to the rest of the group. Musical styles could include opera, reggae or Bollywood.

Warm Up the Worshippers

Divide your group into two teams and pick a well-known song. Stand the two teams opposite each other. The teams must then sing every other word of the song, so that the baton of words passes back and forth from one team to the other.

Keep on Singing

You will need:

✳ CD player and a well-known song

Pick a volunteer from your group. Play a well-known song whilst the volunteer sings along. Turn the song volume down and allow the volunteer to keep singing. When the sound is reintroduced see if they have kept in time and in key!

Foot and Mouth Art

You will need:

✳ Paper
✳ Pencils
✳ Lots of floor space

Get everyone to draw an object or a model, but say they have to do it without using their hands. They can use their feet or mouth to hold pencils and draw. Give them a time limit and see who does the best drawing.

Look, No Hands

You will need:

* A selection of food
* Knives and forks
* Some string (optional)

Again, the object is to not use your hands. There are two ways you can do this. You could just have people hold their hands together behind their backs. If they don't, they must pay a forfeit – they will have to eat something without using their hands.

Alternatively, tie their hands with string. The game is to get people to use their feet to operate the knife and fork, and feed one another. Make sure everyone washes their feet for hygiene reasons, and enjoy a fun meal.

Shakespeare in Love

You will need:

* Paper
* Pens
* A Shakespearean sonnet
* Bowl or container

Read out the sonnet. Hand out a pen and piece of paper to everyone in the group. Each person must write their own love poem, in Shakespearean style – but just four lines long. These are to be folded up and placed in a bowl or container. Say that each person will have an opportunity to take out a piece of paper (not their own) and must read it out to the group as dramatically as possible. They must then guess who wrote it.

Tip: Choose the first person to read out the sonnet wisely... they will set the tone for how dramatic everyone else will be.

Lovely Legs

Ask for five volunteers to stand in a line and show their legs (ankle to knee) to the rest of the group. Ask for another volunteer to study them for a minute. The volunteer should then be blindfolded, and the five people shuffled around. Whilst blindfolded, the volunteer can be given an opportunity to feel each person's legs and guess whose they are.

Brussels Sprout Relaunch

Break the group into small teams and read the following instructions to them:

'You are the marketing adviser to supermarkets, and it concerns you that the Brussels sprout is not achieving the popularity it deserves, especially among children. Your task, should you choose to accept it, is to devise a relaunch campaign for the Brussels sprout, including whatever you think would elevate the Brussels sprout back to its rightful place.'

Allocate ten minutes for each team to come up with their marketing strategy, and get them to present their product relaunch to the rest of the group.

Best Memories

You will need:

* Paper
* Pens
* A hat

Get each person to (anonymously) write their best memories on a piece of paper and to then place it into a hat. Each person should pick a piece of paper from the hat, act out that memory and what they think that person felt. Get the real person to own up and talk about how they really felt.

Fashion Icon

You will need:

* Plenty of newspaper
* Sticky tape
* Odd accessories (for example, feathers, string, cardboard and so on)

In teams of two or three, get people to make an outfit out of newspaper, tape and any of the accessories you have brought. The objective is to design a fashion outfit which one of the people on the team will model to the rest of the group. One person will need to explain what inspired the team, why it is the must-have outfit of the season, and why they made it that way.

Connected Circle

You will need:

* A black sack
* Blindfolds

Get each person to bring along an extra pair of trousers or an extra shirt. Put all the clothes in a black sack. Blindfold half the group and get each blindfolded person to take an item of clothing from the sack. The group should then attempt to form a connected circle by wearing the trousers and shirts, sharing either an arm or a leg with the person next to them. Blindfolded people will need assistance, and clothing can be swapped if it doesn't fit.

VIPs

Ask the group to start thinking of the most important person in their life. Then ask them to come up with three ways in which they can improve that relationship.

Family Circle

You will need:

* A picture board

Prepare a picture board with some human figures stuck on with Blu-tack. Say that each figure represents the family circle. Give each group member an opportunity to pick a figure to represent themselves, and to arrange the other figures according to the closeness of the relationships. You can follow this up with a discussion on the topic.

The Ladder of Life

Prepare a picture with a person in a hole, and someone standing at the top of the hole with a ladder in their hand. Then, ask your group: 'Who would you most and least like to hand you the ladder?' Point out that this picture is a metaphor of the troubles we encounter in life.

Face-Off

Get everyone to face a partner and yell 'Speak!' Everyone will start speaking at one another at the same time, and whoever stops speaking or laughs loses! Winners can pair up again until there is only one person left.

Pairs Eat

You will need:

* A plate of spaghetti Neapolitan per two people
* Blindfold
* Kitchen facilities

Get everyone to choose a partner. Blindfold each pair and ask them to wash their hands in order to feed one another with their hands. The challenge is to see which team can finish the food first. Be careful, this is a messy one!

Chair Flex

You will need:

* A chair
* A pen

This icebreaker will especially interest youth. Grab a sturdy chair and place a pen on the ground at 90 degrees from the back right chair leg. The person must sit on the chair facing forward and lift their feet off the ground. They cannot touch the ground again with any part of their body until they have picked up the pen in their mouth. They must go around the chair from the left side, negotiating the back – it's a combination of balance and flexibility!

Jelly Bean Challenge

You will need:

* Jelly beans with several different flavours

Divide the group into teams. Get each team to send their first delegate to receive a jelly bean from you, to chew it, and go back to their team. The team must guess the flavour of the jelly bean by smelling the delegate's breath! Work through the flavours with different people as delegates.

Eating Relay

You will need:

* Fruit string or fruit laces
* A packet of Hula Hoops

Divide the group into teams, tie four or five fruit strings together and thread the Hula Hoops onto the laces, spreading them out evenly. Two volunteers must hold the string up, each holding an end in their teeth. The other members of the team should then race to eat all of the Hula Hoops off the lace relay-style, with team members going one at a time, and only eating one Hula hoop per trip. When all of the hoops are eaten, the two string holders eat the string towards each other. The winning team is the one who eats all of their string and hoops first!

Sticky Sweets Relay

You will need

* A selection of sweets that are wrapped and get sticky when wet (like hard-boiled sweets)
* A bucket of water
* A chair

Divide the group into teams and appoint one person to be the 'collector'. Teams should be set at one end of the relay line, with wrapped sweets and a bucket of water at the other end. The teams have to run to the sweets, take one, unwrap it, dip it in the water, and run back to the 'collector' who is at the front of the line sitting on a chair. They must stick the sweet to their face. The team with the most sweets stuck to the face of their 'collector' wins. Sweets that are dropped cannot be picked up again.

Extreme Texting

You will need:

* Pieces of paper with text messages on them
* Mobile phones

Give everyone a piece of paper with a difficult text message written on it. The object is for each person to type the text into their mobile phone as quickly as possible and to send it to you. The first text through to your mobile wins. Use different languages such as Greek, Hebrew, Spanish and numbers and symbols to increase the difficulty! You can also do pictures made out of symbols.

Glove Mayhem

You will need:

* Pairs of unused, clean garden gloves
* A bag of chocolate coins or foil-wrapped chocolates per team

Get the group into teams. Each person can have a go at wearing the gloves, unwrapping the chocolate, eating it and passing on the gloves to the next team member until the chocolate is fully consumed. The first team to eat all of their chocolate wins.

Championship Glove Mayhem

Similar to 'Glove Mayhem' but instead of doing a relay you can do a time challenge, where people are timed to see who can put on the gloves, unwrap the chocolate, eat it and show their empty mouth the fastest. You can even have head-to-head elimination matches to see who can handle the extra pressure!

It's a Spoon Thing

You will need:

* A bowl of any food of your choice per pair

Ask each person to bring the biggest spoon that they can find. Pair people up and get them to feed one another the bowl of food with their arms straight at all times. Fun things to feed include jelly, ice cream, rice pudding, cereal, M&M's or even cheese puffs/cheese balls. The winning team is the one who finishes the bowl first.

Energizers

... they will run and not grow weary'.
Isaiah 40:31 (NIV)

We have probably all been to a conference or meeting where there has been a lunch break. Known to some as the 'graveyard shift', the session after lunch can be one of the more difficult times to keep people motivated... and awake! People seem to get really sluggish, as if they need an afternoon sleep – it must be the digestive process kicking in! Others even end up dozing off. This chapter is all about getting sleepy people active, awake and running around. To combat the 'graveyard shift' or to inject some energy into a small group meeting, try using an Energizer!

5 Tips to Run an Energizer

1 If you fail to prepare, you prepare to fail.

2 Know your audience: Do not pick an Energizer that people cannot take part in due to physical limitations.

3 Know your venue: Make sure there is enough space to avoid people bumping into one another.

4 People can get rather loud when running around; if you need amplification to run the Energizer effectively, organize it beforehand.

5 As silly as it may sound, if the Energizer is really physical, get the participants to stretch beforehand as a part of the exercise.

Who's the King of the Jungle?

You will need:

* Chairs
* Cushion

Get everyone to sit in a circle on chairs except for one person who must sit on a cushion. The cushion is the 'hippo', and the chair to the right of the cushion is the 'lion'. All of the other chairs are allocated various animal names (elephant, giraffe, warthog and so on). Each animal has its own name and actions. For example, the lion's noise could be to 'roar' and its action could be clawing. The lion should start the game by making its noise and doing its action. Then the lion must imitate one of the other animal's noise and action. That animal must then respond with its own action and noise, and must either repeat the lion's noise and action, or select another animal to imitate. The group should continue this, picking up the pace as they go, until someone makes a mistake. At this point, the person who made the mistake can be demoted to the hippo's cushion. The whole group can shift up one space towards the lion's chair. The aim of the game is to work your way up to the lion's seat and stay there.

Pop Goes the... Balloon

You will need:

* Balloons

Give each member a balloon to blow up. They have one minute to think of a unique way to burst it, and then given the opportunity to demonstrate this to the group. The winner is decided by the group.

Burst your Bubble!

You will need:

* 1 balloon per person
* String

You will need a large room and lots of energy! Each person must blow up a balloon and, with a piece of string, tie it to their ankle. The aim is to pop another person's balloon whilst defending your own balloon. Great for seeing the competitors come out of their shell!

Bobsleigh

You will need:

* A beacon

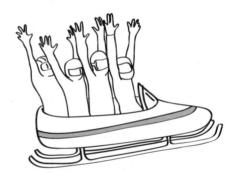

Divide the group into teams of no more than six. The teams must sit on the floor in a straight line, wrapping their legs around the teammate in front of them. Place one beacon 8 metres away from the starting line. Using their hands to drag themselves along, let one team at a time go around the beacon and back. The team with the quickest time wins.

Hide and Seek

The old childhood classic! One person, selected to be the 'seeker', must stand in a corner of the house/garden and begin to count to thirty. Each member should then dash away and hide in a place so as not to be discovered. Once the 'seeker' has finished counting, they yell 'Ready or not, here I come!' and begin their search for the 'hiders'. Whoever is discovered first must run past the 'seeker' to the place where the 'seeker' first counted, without being physically caught, and yell 'SAFE!' If, however, they are caught, the 'seeker' yells 'Game over!' and the group reassembles. The caught 'hider' then becomes the next 'seeker'. The game should continue till you call an end.

Human Maggot Racing

You will need:

* Some sleeping bags

The group is divided into teams of two and each group is given a sleeping bag. The teams must decide who will be the 'human maggot' first. Each 'human maggot' is to climb into their sleeping bag and lie down on the ground with feet touching the starting point, and wait for you or another leader to shout 'Go!'. Once the prompt is given, the 'human maggots' must then 'worm' their way to the finishing line which will be at the opposite end of the room. Hands must be kept in the sleeping bag at all times! The winner is, naturally, the first person to finish. The race is then repeated with the second team member, and then the winners must race to see who the final 'maggot with the most' is. Great for a laugh!

Bottleneck

Divide the group up into four teams, sending each team to a corner of the room. The purpose of the game is for each team to get to the opposite corner of the room before the other teams. The catch is that you decide how the teams will get there. For example, you could call out 'Human wheelbarrow!' You can imagine the massive bottleneck in the middle of the room! The team to reach the opposite corner first is the winner. Here are some other examples: Bunny hopping, crab walking, blindfolded, crawling or even rolling!

Wriggling Mass

Arrange everyone so that they are all at least one metre away from each other. You or another leader can call out a number. The people must group together according to the number called out; no more, no less. Those people who are not grouped according to the number are out the game. When two people are left, they are the winners.

Fruit Salad

You will need:

* Chairs

Arrange the group in a circle on chairs. Make sure there is one chair missing so that one person has to stand in the middle. Whisper into the ear of each person 'apple' or 'banana' or 'pear'. Then the person in the middle (they are also an apple, banana or pear) should call out 'apple' or 'banana' or 'pear'. If they call out apple, all the people who are apples need to swap chairs; they cannot sit back down on their chair or the chair next to them. In the frenzy of chair-finding, you, as the leader, must also attempt to find a chair. The person left in the middle calls again. You can also call 'Fruit salad', which means that everyone has to find a new chair. Total chaos!

Cross Wire

You will need:

* 2 ladders
* A rope
* Safety mat/s

This icebreaker is a fantastic team building exercise. Set up two ladders. Attach a rope to one ladder and run it to the other, attaching it at about five feet above the ground. Make sure there is a safety mat or mats carefully positioned. Now, without touching the rope or the ladder, each team needs to go over the rope to the other side. You may not go underneath it, you must go over it. Time penalties should be given for touching the rope. See who can do it in the quickest time!

Big Knickers Relay

* **Big knickers (XXL or more)**
* **Beacons**
* **Chairs**
* **Tables**

Prepare a relay course, which could include a table to crawl under, beacons to zigzag through... get your imagination juices flowing! Pair up all of the players and then divide the pairs into relay teams. Give each team a pair of big knickers. Each pair is to put the knickers on, one leg around one player's waist and the other leg around the other player's waist. The team must then do the course laid out in relay style; when each pair has completed it, they should to return to their relay line and hand over to the next pair. This can continue until all players have completed the course. Once every pair in the relay team has done so, they should sit down. The first team sitting is the winner.

Spoon on a String

* **A spoon per team**
* **2 m long piece of string per team**

Attach the spoon to the string. Each team must line up so that every person except the front person is facing a player's back. The aim of the game is to get the spoon from the front of the line to the back with the spoon going from the top (blouse or shirt) of clothing to the bottom (trousers). The first person is to hold tightly of the end of the string. The first team to complete this with every player and have the spoon on show is the winner.

Mummy It

* Toilet rolls
* Accessories (for example, cowboy hats and so on)

Divide into teams and give a toilet roll or two to each team. The object is to make one person from each team into a mummy. You can set themes too, such as a cowboy mummy; they must adapt the mummy to match the style.

Iced T-Shirts

* A T-shirt per team
* Plastic sheets for the floor
* Buckets of water (optional)
* Clean towel/change of clothing for members who wear the T-shirts

Wet the T-shirts and twist them into a tight ball (one per team). Place each of them into a bag and freeze overnight so that the T-shirts are completely frozen. Take the T-shirts out of the freezer just before you are ready to play. Put plastic sheets on the floor. The aim is for each team to prise their T-shirt open, and for one member to put on the shirt. Beware: this icebreaker is very physical and wet! Stay away from electrics. If it seems to be taking too long, give each team buckets of water to use to work the ice off.

Stretch Time

This is an easy Energizer to get people active after lunch. Simply put together a series of sports stretches and get the group to follow you in the stretches. Make sure that people do it slowly; get them to do some gentle running on the spot, or sit-ups. This gets the blood flowing and wakes people up for that final push. Enjoy!

The Lace Race

You will need:

＊ **Strawberry laces**

Get the group to form two teams, and then give each member three strawberry laces which they have to tie together, end to end, to create one long strawberry lace. The object of the game is for each member of the two teams to take their strawberry lace to the front and, at the word 'Go!', eat it without using their hands. The next pair must then step forward, with the game continuing until you have a winning team. It is fun, fast-moving and disgusting, depending on your view of strawberry laces!

Scoop a Smartie

You will need:

＊ **2 dishes**

＊ **2 teaspoons**

＊ **Smarties or raisins**

＊ **Table**

Set up a table with two bowls containing Smarties or raisins, and two teaspoons. Divide the group into two teams with each team being allocated a bowl. The object of the game is for a member of each team to race up to their bowl, pick up the teaspoon without using their hands, and to scoop only one Smartie or raisin from the bowl. They must then eat it and race/crawl back to their team, then the next team member sets off. The winners are the team who finish all of the Smarties or raisins first. No cheating allowed!

Write a Song Using Specific Words

Divide into teams and ask them to come up with a song containing random words such as 'gravy' and 'itchy'. Then share with the group.

Newspaper Snake

You will need:

* Newspaper
* A timer

This can be done as a group or individually. Give each group or person a piece of newspaper. At the word 'Go!' they have X number of minutes (usually two or three minutes) to tear the piece of newspaper into the longest continuous piece possible. The group or person with the longest piece wins.

Blind Taste Test

You will need:

* Blindfolds
* Assorted desserts
* Sweets or chocolates
* Paper and pens (optional)

Blindfold each person in the group and get them to taste and identify each dessert, sweet or chocolate. They can even write it down on a piece of paper whilst blindfolded. It is quite fun because they do not know what to expect and usually think that it is something nasty that they are being made to taste.

Moving Chairs

You will need:

* Chairs

People should sit in a circle on chairs, with one person standing in the middle. The person in the middle must make a statement such as 'Football is a brilliant sport!' Everyone who agrees with the statement has to stand up and run to another seat, including the person standing in the middle. The person who does not manage to get a chair is left standing in the middle and has to be the next person to make a statement.

Have You Ever

✳ **Chairs**

One person must sit on a chair in the middle of the group and ask a question which starts with, 'Have you ever...?' They themselves should be able to answer 'Yes' to the question. If the answer applies to anyone else, they should get up and swap seats (including the person who asked the question, so someone else will be in the middle). The person in the middle must now ask the next question. Here are some suggested questions:

● Have you ever climbed to the highest point in your country of birth?

● Have you ever lived overseas for more than one year?

● Have you ever sung karaoke?

● Have you ever been without a shower for more than two weeks?

● Have you ever ridden a horse?

Dancerobics

✳ **Music**

Easy dance aerobics. Someone can lead and the whole group follow. Dance to a funky tune. You can rotate the leader so that it goes around the circle with everyone doing a move, and everyone else following.

Newspaper Tents

✳ **Newspaper**
✳ **Masking tape**

Use for camping theme events. Supply newspaper and masking tape. Have teams build tents out of newspaper – the tent must be large enough for one person to sleep inside. You can set a time limit (fifteen minutes is recommended).

Popcorn Tossing

You will need:

* Popcorn

Have some people be the catchers, and ask others to be the throwers. The aim is to see how many pieces of popcorn the thrower manages to get into the catcher's mouth.

Gorilla, Hunter, Lady!

Similar to paper, rock, scissors, but you act out the Gorilla, hunter or lady with your whole body. Come up with your own actions. Divide everyone into pairs, who must then compete against each other. The winning person from each pair must compete against another pair's winning person until you are left with the final two. Last one standing wins. The Gorilla is killed by the hunter, the hunter swoons to the lady, and the ape takes the lady away!

S-I-N-G

You will need:

* A table
* Straws
* Ping-pong balls

Get your small group around a table (round or oval is best). Give everyone a straw and place a ping-pong ball in the middle of the table. The object is to blow the ball off the table, but not to let the ball fall off your side of the table. Note: the table should be clear and no bodies should be touching it! If the ball goes out at someone's section of the table they must be given a letter, starting with 'S' then 'I' and so on. If it falls off the table between them and the person next to them then they both get a letter. If they get enough letters to spell S-I-N-G, then they must sing a song for everyone, and the game should then continue.

Malteser Blow Ball

You will need:

* Some Maltesers

Get people to try and blow their Malteser as high as they can just using their mouths.

Malteser Blow Football

You will need:

* Some Maltesers
* Table

Using a table and a Malteser for a football, set up a tournament; players can only win if they manage to blow the Malteser off of their opponent's end of the table. Note, no straws allowed.

Malteser Football

You will need:

* Some Maltesers
* Straws
* Table or tray

Create a mini football pitch with a tray or table or something similar and use a Malteser as a football. Create goal posts on either side (possibly using the straws). Create two teams and arm each player with a straw. The teams will use the straw to blow the Malteser ball into their respective goals.

Extreme Freeze

You will need:

✳ **Socks and ice cream tubs for preparation**

✳ **Hammers**

Freeze individual socks in plastic ice cream tubs with water. Remove the tubs from the freezer as close to the icebreaker as you can, and extract the solid 'sock' ice blocks. Bring the same number of hammers as ice blocks. The competition is to see who can get the sock out the quickest! You can make it harder by doing it in a relay, where everyone has to run 20 metres to the ice block and are only allowed one swing before they run back and tag the next person. If the sock is freed, the one who swung the last blow can't take the sock – the next person has to.

Kinder Surprise

You will need:

✳ **Kinder Surprise eggs**

✳ **A prize for the winner**

Each person is to bring a Kinder Surprise egg with them. Eat the eggs together, build the toys found on the inside and keep the plastic egg holder ('the missile') that the toys come in. Mix the big and small toys up and place them in a straight line on the carpet. Stand a good distance away from the toys (such as three to five metres). Take turns to throw the 'missiles' at the toys, trying to knock as many of them over as possible. Tally up each person's points (knocking over a large toy gains two points; knocking over a small toy gains five points). The prize for the winner is all of the toys.

Musical Questions

You will need:

* Chairs
* Music

Get to know one another better. This game is similar to musical chairs. Place chairs in a circle – there must be one less chair than there are people present. Everyone should stand in a circle in the middle of the circle. Music can be played and everyone must run around inside the circle. When the music stops, everyone needs to take a seat. The person left standing in the middle of the circle must pick someone who can ask them a question about themselves. Once they have answered the question, the music should start playing and everyone begin running around again. Keep playing until everyone has had an opportunity to answer at least one question about themselves.

Toe Tramping

Everyone in the group should find a partner. They then lock hands and begin to try and tap their partner's toe with their foot. Avoid crushing their toes. The first to get three taps wins and goes on to the next round!

Taste the Food

You will need:

* Blindfolds
* A selection of food, such as lemon, onion, prawns, potato or liver

Everyone is blindfolded. The selection of food is displayed in the middle of a table. Each person has to take something from the table and eat it.

Water
Challenge

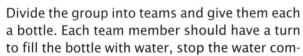

You will need:

❋ **An empty 2-litre water bottle that has twelve holes strategically spaced around it – 1 bottle per team**

❋ **Buckets**

Divide the group into teams and give them each a bottle. Each team member should have a turn to fill the bottle with water, stop the water coming out by covering the holes with their fingers as best they can, and then run to the bucket and empty the water they have in the bottle, before running back to their team. The next team member must do the same. Give them a time limit of about five minutes to try and fill the bucket up. The winning team is the one with the most water in the bucket at the end.

The Blind Line

You will need:

❋ **10m rope**
❋ **Blindfolds**

Take the group to a public place where there is a lot of space to walk. Form a line with each member approximately one metre apart, holding the rope. All team members must be blindfolded except the person leading the party. The object is to go for a fifteen-minute walk with the leader guiding the group around and over all obstacles. The communication should be passed on down the line, making sure that nobody stumbles. As soon as someone stumbles the leader must lose their position to the person behind, and go to the back of the line and be blindfolded.

Not a Drop

You will need:

* Cups
* Water
* Trays
* Blindfolds

Divide the group into teams of two standing approximately five metres apart. One team member is blindfolded. The blindfolded person has to carry a cup of water filled to the brim on a tray to their team mate without spilling it. This can be adapted to bigger groups with a relay.

Musical Cushions

You will need:

* Music
* Cushions

Take the group to a public place. Each member should bring a cushion. The game works the same as musical chairs, only the cushions get removed instead of chairs when the music stops.

Drummers Unite

You will need:

* A selection of percussion instruments, for example, a coffee tin, a water drum or a bottle full of pebbles

Give each person a percussion instrument of sorts. Come up with creative beats, giving people a chance to go 'solo' on their instrument. Build up the beats slowly, with each person doing a different beat, but keep the same rhythm.

Rearranging

People get very stuck in the way they do things, especially over a long period of time. Get the group to totally rearrange the seating. Make sure that no one person is sitting next to the person they were sitting next to previously!

Clothes Pegs Relay

You will need:

* **Pegs**

Divide the group into teams. Give each team ten clothes pegs. Attach the pegs to one member of each group. They have to run around a certain point and, upon returning, the next person has to remove the pegs with their mouth before reattaching the pegs to themselves. The first team to finish wins.

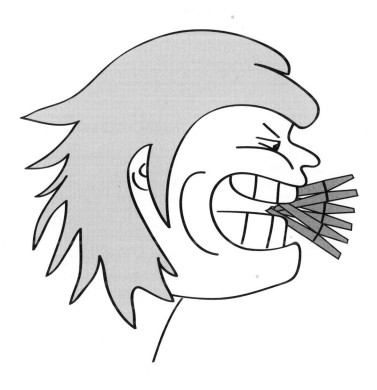

Getting the Word In

'Then you will know the truth, and the truth will set you free.'
John 8:32 (NIV)

Icebreakers are not just about running around, making a noise or having extreme amounts of fun. They are a tool to help foster community, to get us talking and relating to one another. This chapter presents a more Word-based set of challenges. Although some of them are really tricky, others are great fun! These icebreakers can be used to give people a rough overview of the Bible, or for the more mature, they can draw out biblical principles for group sessions.

5 Tips for Getting the Word In

1   If you fail to prepare, you prepare to fail.

2   Make sure everyone has a Bible; otherwise people can feel left out. Organize a few extra copies for potential need.

3   Pair up strong people with weaker people. In this way, those who are totally new to the Bible will not feel too intimidated by the knowledge of others.

4   Do your own research beforehand: You need to be able to lead the discussion where you feel it should go.

5   Test everything people come up with: Just because they read the Word does not mean they interpret it correctly!

Alphabet Names

You will need:

✳ **Paper**

✳ **Pens**

Divide everyone into groups. Without the use of their Bibles, each group should write down a name from the Bible for each letter of the alphabet, for example, A-Adam, J-Joshua, X-Xerxes.

Book by Verse

You will need:

✳ **Paper**

✳ **Pens**

Divide everyone into groups. Without the use of their Bibles, each group should write down one verse from each book of the Bible. The group with the most verses wins.

The Word

You will need:

✳ **Paper**

✳ **Pens**

Divide everyone into groups. Without the use of their Bibles, each group should write down as much of the Bible as they can. Give them a twenty minute time limit!

What is a Father?

You will need:

✳ Whiteboard and pen
✳ Concordances (optional)

Write the word 'Father' on a whiteboard. Each person must research the word 'Father' in the Bible. See what comes out. Use this time to discuss how people view 'fathers' in different ways. (Be aware that this could cause some issues with people who have not had good experiences of fatherhood, so be sensitive.)

Bible Names Challenge

You will need:

✳ A concordance

One member should start by saying a character's name from the Bible, for example, 'Abraham'. The person to their right can then use the last letter of that name to start another name, for example, Mary. If they cannot say a name in the time given (about three seconds), they are 'out'. The game should continue until there is a battle between two. Whoever is left last is the winner. (The concordance is to verify the name exists.)

Fruits of the Spirit

You will need:

✳ Paper
✳ Pens

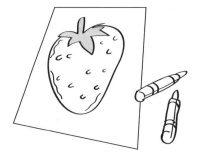

Simply read through the fruits of the Spirit in Galatians 5:22–23. Get each person to draw a picture that illustrates one of the fruits. Once everyone has finished, they can explain their picture to the group.

Director's Cut

Divide the group into teams of at least four and ask each team to act out a story from the Bible in one minute. Give them ten to fifteen minutes to prepare. Examples could include the beheading of John the Baptist, Samson and Delilah and the tower of Babel. You also have the option of adding the style in which it needs to be presented such as opera, rap or Shakespearean English.

Creation?

People always have trouble remembering what happened on what day during the creation! Divide everyone into seven groups, one for each day of creation. Suggest they act out in sequence the events of the creation.

The Big Ten

You will need:

* Paper
* Pens

This icebreaker is similar to the one above. In this one, do not act out the Ten Commandments, but rather get each group to write and perform a song that will remind people of the order.

Psalm Writing

You will need:

* Paper
* Pens

Choose a collection of psalms from the Bible and read them out to the group. Get each person in the group to write their own psalm in line with what you have read. Give them fifteen minutes to do this. Once everyone has finished, get them to read their psalm as a prayer.

Passage Parody

You will need:

✳ Dressing up clothes

✳ Props

Divide everyone into groups of three, and give each group a parable or story from the Bible. Each group must enact the passage that they have been given, but they are to use a film genre such as western, sci-fi, silent film, love story or cartoon. Encourage the groups to dress up and to use props.

Most-Wanted Verse

Get each person in the group to share their favourite Bible verse with the group. Ask them why it is their favourite. Who have they shared it with lately, and who are they going to share it with this coming week?

Biblical Food

Look through the Bible for all references pertaining to food. Come up with a diet from the Bible.

Verse Countdown!

You will need:

✳ Key words, written on pieces of paper

✳ Hat or bowl

Beforehand, write key words in the Bible on separate pieces of paper, fold them and place them into a hat or bowl. The members of the group should be divided into two teams. Upon instruction, each group must pick a word and, without looking at it, wait for you or another leader to say 'Go!'. Then the groups need to come up with as many verses in the Bible that contain that key word. The group with the most verses at the end is the winner.

Mission Madness

Discuss the following:

● What are missions all about? Are we supposed to go on missions, and if so, what should we do? Look through the book of Acts to see what it says about missions.

One at a Mime Please!

Get each person to choose a story from the Bible and give them one minute to mime it to the group. The group must then guess what the story is.

Build a Warrior

You will need:

✳ **Black sacks**

✳ **Paper**

✳ **Sticky tape**

✳ **Blu-tack**

✳ **String**

✳ **Large cardboard boxes**

✳ **Crayons**

Divide the group into teams of about three, and give each group a black sack, paper, sticky tape, Blu-tack, string, a large cardboard box and crayons. Their challenge is to build the best 'Ephesians 6' warrior they can, and describe why this warrior is better than all of the others.

Not Just Tasty Fruit

You will need:

* A selection of different kinds of fruit
* Fruit knife

Ask each person to choose a piece of fruit. Ask them why they chose it, and what they like about it. Ask them what they see when they look at the fruit. Then take an apple and cut it in half, showing everyone the seeds. This can set the scene for a discussion about the following topics:

● Leadership: It is within each one of us, although it can be dormant. The potential is there, but are we going to plant it, nurture it and see it grow, or are we going to throw it away, never fulfilling its purpose?

● Reproducing: A seed becomes a tree that in turns bears a fruit with seed in it. The seed is about potential; are we going to invest in the next generation by planting and sowing into their lives?

Topical Topping Pizza

You will need:

* Pizza bases
* Kitchen facilities

Contact your group beforehand to ask them to bring their favourite pizza toppings. These can be either sweet or savoury.

Get the group to make pizzas together and to come up with different varieties. Once the pizzas are made, put them in the oven and get together for a group discussion on the following:

● Foundations: The pizza is great with all the toppings, but take away the base and you have nothing *but* toppings! Likewise, one needs a strong, firm foundation to life and faith.

● Body: The body is a unit and we are all individually and uniquely made, each with the same importance as the other. God has created us to be the body of Christ, and in that body we need different parts – we cannot all be an arm, as a collection of arms does not make up a body (1 Corinthians 12:12–31).

Cake Head

You will need:

* **Cake mix**

* **Eggs**

* **Water**

* **Oil**

* **Icing**

Give the group some cake mix, eggs, water, oil and icing. Select somebody who doesn't mind getting messy, and get the others to mix the ingredients of the cake directly onto the person's head. Then discuss the following:

● We can have all the right ingredients in our lives, church, youth, small groups, mentoring, but if we haven't got the right foundation the rest is useless.

Invention

You will need:

* **A pile of 'junk' – random items such as cereal boxes, cartons, buttons**

* **Pens**

* **Crayons**

* **Paint**

Divide your group into smaller teams and give each one a selection of random items. Allocate ten minutes to make something artistic out of them. Then get the teams together and discuss the following:

● God can and will use the 'junk' in our lives, if we allow him to, for something of purpose and of beauty. You are precious to him even with all your 'junk', and he will use you, and turn your life around to bring glory himself.

Purpose?

People are always speaking about their purpose in God. What does the Word say about our purpose? Or is it *his* purpose in our lives?

Biblical Twister

You will need:

* 2 'Twister' board games

* A number of biblical questions for each team

Divide the group into two teams and nominate a leader from each team. The usual rules for the game 'Twister' apply, except that the team that spins answers a biblical question from the opposing team, which the team leader reads out. If they answer the question correctly they don't have to move, but the opposing team does. The winner is the team with the last person standing.

Know His Voice

You will need:

* Audio clips of famous musicians, singers, entertainers, actors

* Paper and pens

Divide the group into teams. Play audio clips of famous people your group will know, and get the teams to write down who they think it is. Upon completion of the quiz, discuss the following:

● How do you recognize God's voice? Are you intimidated by him? Do you have a deep relationship with him?

Red Letter Message

Select a passage from one of the Gospels from a red-letter edition of the Bible. Get the people in the group to read this passage, but do not read any of the black text, only read the words of Jesus. You will be amazed at what he says!

Jesus' Lineage

Look at the lineage of Jesus in Matthew 1. Try to find a scriptural reference to every person mentioned in this passage.

Remembrance

We all struggle to remember the order of the books in the Old Testament. Divide the group into teams. Get each team to present a drama, song or piece of art to help people remember the order. (This can be done for both Old and New Testaments.)

Memory Circle

To help us remember the books of the Bible, arrange the group into a circle. Allow the group to study the order of the books of the Bible for five minutes. Pick somebody to start with any book in the Bible. Go around the circle with each following person saying the next book. For example, start at Philippians, go through to Revelation, back to Genesis and end at Ephesians. Do this a number of times starting with different books and different people.

Worship

You will need:

✳ **Concordances**

Using the concordances, get the group to look at all the references to the words 'Praise' and 'Worship' in the Bible. Write down all of the different meanings of these words. Now, have a time of praise and worship, without music and only using the actions you have just learned about.

Bible Challenge

This icebreaker is a race. Each person must place their Bible on their head. Then give a scripture reference; the first one to find it wins a point. Alternatively, give each person a verse without a scripture reference. They have to find the reference. The first person (or team) to find it wins a point.

You can also test whether each person can say the books of the Bible (or the books of the Old or New Testament) either backwards or forwards.

Draw a Bible Story (much like Pictionary)

You will need:

✳ **Whiteboard and pens**

Split the group into two teams. Get one team to draw a Bible story whilst the other team guesses which it is. They can take turns to guess and draw.

Seven Habits

Challenge the group: Think of seven habits that you have in your life. Can these habits be backed up by the Word? If so, share these scriptures, and if not, what does the Word say about them?

What's True and What's Not True?

Present the group with a list of Bible facts, some of which should be true, some slightly questionable and some blatant lies. The group must then guess which statements are true and which are not. This can be done individually or in a group.

Bible Team Challenge

In teams, find out the longest and shortest book, chapter, and/or verse in the Bible. Pick a scripture based on the theme of your meeting and create a crossword for it with clues. This can be used to launch into a discussion around the chosen scripture. Alternatively, get people into teams to find as many scriptures as they can on the theme or topic of your meeting. Give either a limited amount of scriptures to find, or limited time in which to find them. As a bonus you could get them to pick a scripture to memorize as a team and recite the next time you meet.

Your Testimony

You will need:

✳ **Paper**
✳ **Pen**

Ask the group if they have ever thought about sharing their testimonies. Get each person to write their testimony – how they came to know Jesus – down. Now, encourage people to weave scripture into their testimony without quoting it.

Headline Challenge

You will need:

✳ **Current newspaper**

Take today's newspaper and insert your own headlines from biblical stories. Space them throughout the newspaper and get the teams to find the headlines and decipher them within a time limit. For example, 'Postcard from Nineveh. Having a whale of a time!' (Jonah); 'King has close call of nature!' (Saul when he relieves himself in the cave and David cut the corner of his robe); 'Strongman brings house down!' (Samson).

Playdough Pictionary

You will need:

* Playdough
* A list of biblical characters

Divide the group into teams of four. Each group should be given a chunk of playdough. You are the 'game master' and hold the list of biblical characters. Each team will nominate a player to come to you to get the name of the first character (this must be done quietly so that the other teams' members can't hear). They must then return to their group and make something out of the playdough to depict this character. No talking allowed! The rest of the team must guess which character they are shaping. Once they have guessed correctly, the team should send another person forward to say what the character's name is, and to find out who the next character is. The winning team will be the first to guess all of the names.

Examples:

● Noah – make a boat

● Jonah – make a fish

● Daniel – make a lion

Bible Hide

Hide scriptures around the venue and do a scripture hunt with your group. When all of the scriptures have been found, get the group to read them out loud. Make sure that the scriptures relate to the theme of the meeting.

Names of God

Sitting in a circle, each person must declare a name for God. Keep going round the circle until no one can think of any more names for God. This can lead into worship or a discussion regarding God's names and character. You can search for scriptures and talk about how we relate to God in different circumstances.

Examples of names of God:

● Jehovah-Jireh

● Jehovah-Shalom

● Shepherd

● Love

● I Am

● Lion of Judah

Musical Scriptures

Divide the group into two teams. Give each team a scripture, preferably something that relates to the theme of the meeting.

Each team must turn their scripture into a song, including actions, which they can perform and teach the other team. Tip: To make it fun, give each team a musical genre to perform it in, such as rhythm and blues or country and western.

Bible Dramatization

Split the group into smaller teams of about four people and give them three minutes to come up with a drama that summarizes the whole Bible in five minutes. Mark them on how much of the Bible they have shown and also on accuracy.

Topic Chooser

Choose a topic from the Word. Get the group to find as many scriptures as they can in reference to this topic. See what comes out!

Psalm Challenge

Split into smaller groups. Choose a psalm from the Bible. Get each group to rewrite the psalm in a certain style, for example, rap, cockney rhyming slang. They must then perform it for the whole group.

Memories

You will need:

* Pens
* Paper

Split the group into two teams. Give each team a book from the Bible that they must memorize as best they can in five minutes. Get the opposing team to come up with ten questions to ask the other team, based on their Bible book. The objective is to get the opposing team to answer as few questions correctly as possible.

The Parables

How many parables are there in the Gospels? Break the group into four teams. Give each team one of the four Gospels. Tell them they must read through the Gospel and search for as many parables as possible.

Miracles

This is a variation of the above game. Do the same thing but find all the miracles that Jesus performed.

Open-Heart Surgery

'Above all else, guard your heart, for it is the wellspring of life.'
Proverbs 4:23 (NIV)

The fun stuff, the laughter and the excitement are great but the time comes when we need to become real with one another. Relationships are not built solely on having a laugh; they grow as we begin to open our lives up to one another. In this chapter you will find icebreakers that challenge people to open their hearts. Use them as a link from a fun time into a more serious time. Remember that they are a tool to get people speaking; some people will find this really difficult. Give them time to grow in it; you will be surprised by the results!

5 Tips for Open-Heart Surgery

1 If you fail to prepare, you prepare to fail.

2 Do not force people to open up, give them time.

3 Be prepared to start in order to set the tone. This means you will need to have your input prepared carefully.

4 If you need to, set a time limit for people's input.

5 Make sure that you encourage and build people up as they are making themselves vulnerable to the group.

Timeline

You will need:

* Paper
* Pens

Ask each member to draw their life on a timeline and to include all significant events, both positive and negative. They can then share with the group if they feel comfortable about doing so.

A Picture of the Week

You will need:

* A4 sheets of paper
* Paint and paintbrushes
* Plenty of tissues

Each member must paint their week and then share about it – get ready for tissue time!

Bag that Item

Each member can be asked to bring along an item and explain to the group why this most reminds them of what God has recently done in their life.

Black and White

Each member can be asked to share a happy/good thing and a sad/unhappy thing that is currently taking place in their lives. (Be aware that this might be quite a sensitive issue for some.)

Fear Factor

You will need:

* Paper
* Pens
* Hat

As people arrive, get each person to write their worst fear on a piece of paper, which is then placed in a hat. Later, get them to draw one piece of paper from the hat. They need to explain what the fear is, and how someone would feel if they experienced that fear. If they draw their own fear, they need to replace it and choose another one.

Influence

Who are the people that have had the greatest influence in your life and why? Go around the group and see how many people were influenced by their parents and how many were not. Use this as a link into speaking about God's influence as a 'Father' in our lives. But be aware that some people might find the whole issue of fatherhood quite difficult to discuss.

Highs and Lows

Get the group to share their greatest and worst moments at both junior and secondary school. This is a great way to see how people view their early years.

Release of Power

Challenge the group: Share a story of forgiveness from your life. Focus on the peace that it released in your life and the restoration that it brought. Note that this icebreaker is meant to encourage people, not to complain about someone else.

Testifying Christ

Challenge the group: What persecution have you had to endure for being a Christian, and how did you respond? Share with people the joy and the struggle that we have when we are a witness to Christ in our lives.

Servanthood Begins After Midnight

We all need to grow in the area of our servanthood. In the Western world we live a fast-paced life, and we often plan months in advance. What are the challenges we face in servanthood when our lives have become so structured?

The Word

Challenge the group: When was the last time you spent quality time studying the Word of God? If you have not formed this discipline in your life, how can you begin to do it? What prevents you from this discipline? Time? Laziness? Apathy?

Hearing from God

Challenge the group: What was the last thing that God spoke to you about?

How to Connect?

All of us have different ways in which we connect with God. For some it is nature; for others it is cleaning the house. How do you connect with God? Get the group to share their way.

Name Markers

You will need:

* Laminated bookmarks

Laminate little bookmarks with each person's name. Research the meaning of their name and, if appropriate, the scriptural reference. This is very special as a lot of people do not know what their names mean. Use this to talk about identity.

Tortilla Time

You will need:

* Candles
* CD player and music
* Mexican food
* Plates

Place lots of candles in the room and play reflective music. Decorate a table with lots of different Mexican food. Each person could make up their favourite tortilla and then once they have done so, they must bless someone else with it. Before they eat they should pray with that person and spend time over the meal chatting.

Six Word Testimony

You will need:

* Paper
* Pens
* CD player and music

Give each person a piece of paper and a pen. Give them ten minutes to think about their life so far. To help in this process, play some soft, thought-provoking music. At the end of the allocated time, get each person to sum up their life in only six words and encourage them to share it with the rest of the group.

J.O.Y.

Ask each person to share three things:

● **J:** Something in your life that JUST happened.

● **O:** ONE thing you would like to do for yourself.

● **Y:** A part of YOU that makes you a very special person.

Listen attentively as each member shares, and encourage each other. End the icebreaker with a prayer session or with worship.

Tree Climbing

You will need:

✱ **A picture of a tree with branches and children climbing either up or down the tree, or just sitting on a branch**

Depending on the size of the group, either stay as one group or split up. Ask them to imagine the tree depicts their relationship with God. Whereabouts on the tree do they feel they are? Encourage them to share thoughts and feelings.

Grave Feelings

You will need:

✱ **A picture of a gravestone with enough space on it for people to write (1 per person attending)**

✱ **Pens**

Get each person to write what they want said about them on their tombstone – how would they like to be remembered?

Looking at Me

You will need:

❋ **Paper**
❋ **Pens**

Get each person to draw three columns on a piece of paper and label them:

● What I think

● What I think others think about me

● What others think

Then ask a series of questions such as 'What are your strengths?', 'Weaknesses?', 'Areas needing improvement?', 'Goals?', 'Future?' Each person should put their answers in the first two columns, but the final column must be left free. Once all of the questions are answered, each person's paper must be folded, leaving just the 'What others think' column facing upwards. The person's name should be on top. Everyone's papers should be passed around, and other people should fill in the final column. Everyone must then take their original paper back and compare the three columns for any discrepancies.

Famous Faces

You will need:

❋ **A selection of famous faces, cut out from magazines and newspapers**

Let everyone pick which part of the famous faces they would choose if they could swap their features for their own. This gives an insight into what people don't like about themselves, and you can lead into a discussion on identity or the way that God sees us.

Time Challenge

Challenge the group: Where do you want to be in five years time, spiritually, emotionally and financially? How are you going to achieve these goals? What are the major challenges that will prevent you from seeing the realization of these goals?

Hurt Feelings

Ask the group to think about a time in their lives when they hurt someone's feelings – or someone hurt *them*. Ask: How did it make you feel, and how did you overcome this problem? Share thoughts and feelings.

Thanksgiving

You will need:

❋ **Paper**
❋ **Pens**

Get the group to write on a piece of paper everything they should be thankful for. Suggest they do not neglect the simple things in life, such as food and clothing. Do this for three or four meetings straight, and each time it will become easier – people are not used to being grateful for what they have!

Prophecy of Jesus

You will need:

❋ **Bibles**

Look through the Old Testament and find as many prophecies about Jesus as possible.

Pandora's Box

'Wisdom will save you from the ways of wicked men...'
Proverbs 2:12a (NIV)

There are many controversial topics out there. In this context, the ideas in this chapter are not expressed with a view to create an argument or controversy, but are to be used as a tool to get people thinking. Many people do not have the ability to construct a logical defence for what they believe. In fact, they are swayed by opinions instead of being rooted in the truth of the Word. This chapter is therefore aimed at getting people to look into the Word for biblical responses to a controversial issue, instead of relying on personal opinions or good ideas.

8 Tips for Pandora's Box

1 If you fail to prepare, you prepare to fail.

2 Know the topic before you speak on it. Therefore be prepared to do some research beforehand.

3 Watch out for conflicts: Pandora's Box is meant to facilitate a discussion rather than orchestrate a battle of wills and opinions.

4 If someone makes a statement or offers some input, ask them to back up what they are proposing with scripture.

5 Test everything people come up with: Just because they read the Word does not mean they interpret it correctly.

6 Watch out that people do not force their opinions onto others.

7 Choose your topic wisely: You do not want to confuse young or immature Christians.

8 Have the last word on the topic. End the discussion on a positive note!

Kick Him Out?

The minister's son is found to have been doing drugs and clubbing every night, but plays the guitar in the worship band. What do you think should happen?

Drunken Leader

You find out that a church leader is addicted to alcohol. What do you think should happen?

He Prefers Men...

One of your work colleagues is interested in becoming a Christian but has one major stumbling block – he is attracted to other men rather than women. Is this genetic? Can he get healed of this? Or, is there no help for him?

Man or Woman?

You lead an Alpha group, and on the fourth week one of your group members, Alison, becomes a Christian. She is single and is looking for a husband. She lets you know that she was really born Allan, and at the age of twenty-eight had a sex change. How does God now see her?

Give advice.

Dating

Dating and courtship? Where in the Bible does it speak about these topics?

Sex Before Marriage (1)

Your friend confides in you that she and her boyfriend are sleeping together. They are both Christians and believe it is right to get married. One night they made a promise before God to stay together for the rest of their lives. As the Bible does not prescribe the specific details of how you get married, they believe that they are now married in the eyes of God. What do you think?

Sex Before Marriage (2)

Your friend laughs when you say you will wait until you are married before you have sex with your boy/girlfriend. He says, 'You wouldn't buy a pair of shoes without trying them on.' Isn't marriage more important than shoes? How do you know if you are sexually compatible?

Give a response.

Sex Before Marriage (3)

A couple in your young persons' group have been going out for two years and are close to getting engaged. You ask them about the physical side of their relationship and they admit to going as far as mutual masturbation but no further. They feel this level of intimacy is appropriate at this stage and they feel closer as a result. Are you happy with this? Why/why not?

Genetic Engineering

A couple have found out that their five-year-old son has a life-threatening blood disorder. They would like to have a specially chosen child with the correct genetic make-up to provide a cure for their son. They were planning to have another child anyway.

What is your advice?

Inconceivably Challenging

A couple who are close friends of yours have been trying to conceive for ten years. You have personally witnessed their heartache. They want your opinion on their recent thoughts: They are considering IVF treatment. Is there a moral problem with using donated sperm? If all this fails, they might consider using a surrogate mother. What are your thoughts?

Abortion (1)

Your best friend, who is a Christian, falls pregnant and wants to have an abortion. What do you say to her?

Abortion (2)

A woman asks your advice on a tough decision she is facing. She was raped two months ago and is now pregnant. The thought of bringing up the rapist's child is too much – she wants an abortion.

Abortion (3)

A woman finds out that she has an ectopic pregnancy and has heard that one or two other women with ectopic pregnancies have gone full term, producing a healthy baby without killing the mother. Should she refuse the doctor's suggestion of an abortion?

Food for Thought

A friend does not eat meat because of the suffering it causes to animals – after all, she says, why should we, who are ourselves animals, kill other animals?

She also asks you if, as a Christian, you should recycle waste?

Give a biblical response.

Animal Lover

Your dog is infested with fleas and you are an animal lover. Can you morally kill one animal (such as a flea) to help another?

A Question of Time

One of your friends asks you, 'How old is the earth if it was created in six days? I know a geography teacher who says the earth is 4.5 billion years old. So how old is it?'

I Don't Adam and Eve It!

Your college friend wants to become a Christian but cannot accept that human beings were created from two people when there is so much evidence to suggest a wide range of 'hominids'. What is your advice?

Meat or Veg?

Genesis 1:30 clearly states, 'to all the beasts of the earth and all the birds of the air and all the creatures that move on the ground... I give every green plant for food' (NIV). If this is the case, where did the sharp teeth for tearing/cutting meat, and the instinct to hunt come from?

A Monster of a Question

Why are dinosaurs not mentioned in the Bible? When were they created and what happened to them?

Away with Animals

How did Noah get all of those animals into the ark? Is it practically possible?

The Problem of Suffering

Get a recent newspaper cutting of a headline or story regarding a current issue, such as the search for a missing child. Get people to share their thoughts. Questions like 'Where is God in all this?' or 'Why does he allow this to happen?' may arise and open up discussion points.

'To know how to use knowledge is to have wisdom.'
Charles Spurgeon

Quiz 1

Q 1. When Lazarus came out of the tomb, what parts of his body were wrapped?
A *His hands, feet and face – John 11:44*

Q 2. How many wives did Moses have?
A *Two, Zipporah and a Cushite woman – Exodus 2:21 and Numbers 12:1*

Q 3. True or false: Abram travelled from Ur with his family.
A *True – Genesis 11:31*

Q 4. How many sons and daughters did Izban have?
A *Thirty of each – Judges 12:9*

Q 5. 'Doubting Thomas' also had another name, what was it?
A *Didymus – John 20:24*

Q 6. Why did Paul leave Titus in Crete?
A *So he could 'straighten out what was left unfinished' (NIV) and appoint elders – Titus 1:5*

Q 7. What was the Temple lampstand adorned with?
A *Almond flowers – Exodus 37:20*

Q 8. Who was the eunuch assigned to Esther?
A *Hathach – Esther 4:5*

Q 9. Why did the Israelites wear tassels on their clothes?
A *To remind them of God's commandments – Numbers 15:39*

Q 10. Why did Priscilla and Aquila move to Corinth?
A *Because Claudius, the emperor, made all the Jews leave Rome – Acts 18:2*

Quiz 2

Q 1. To whom did God say 'I will heal you… I will add fifteen years to your life'?
A   Hezekiah via Isaiah – 2 Kings 20:5-6

Q 2. What was Achan's sin?
A   He took some devoted things from Jericho – Joshua 7:1

Q 3. What was the Ethiopian eunuch reading when he met Phillip?
A   The book of Isaiah – Acts 8:28

Q 4. Methuselah lived longer than anyone else recorded in the Bible. Who came in second?
A   Jared, Methuselah's grandfather – Genesis 5:20

Q 5. James and John were the sons of Zebedee, but who was their mother?
A   Salome – Mark 15:40

Q 6. Why did Paul shave his head?
A   It marked the end of a vow he had taken – Acts 18:18

Q 7. Who, as a king, tried to hire Balaam to curse Israel?
A   Balak – Numbers 22:4-6

Q 8. Who was the commander of Saul's army that died by being stabbed in the stomach by Joab?
A   Abner – 2 Samuel 3:27

Q 9. During the Passover, what were the Israelites instructed not to break?
A   The bones of their feast – Exodus 12:46

Q 10. How many did Jesus choose to travel ahead of him in pairs to heal people?
A   Seventy-two – Luke 10:1

Quiz 3: SUPERHERO IDENTITIES AND POWERS

Q 1. Bananaman
A Eric Twinge: Banana-eating turns schoolboy into superhero

Q 2. Batman
A Bruce Wayne: Martial arts, gadgets

Q 3. Captain America
A Steve Rogers: Strength – super-soldier serum

Q 4. Dan Dare
A Colonel Daniel, MacGregor Dare: Good pilot

Q 5. Daredevil
A Matt Murdock: Martial arts, sonar

Q 6. The Flash
A Jay Garrick, or Barry Allen, or Wally West: Superhuman speed

Q 7. He-man
A Prince Adam: Strength, He-man has a pet cat named Cringer who becomes Battle Cat

Q 8. The Hulk
A Robert Bruce Banner: Strength, aggression

Q 9. Judge Dredd
A Joe Dredd: Combat skills, gadgets

Q 10. The Phantom
A Kit Walker, or Sir Christopher Standish: No supernatural powers

Q 11. The Shadow
A Lamont Cranston, or Kent Allard: Master of disguise, shooting ability

Q 12. Spider-Man
A Peter Parker: Web-making, enhanced senses

Q 13. Supergirl
A Linda Lee Danvers: Strength, flight

Q 14. Superman
A Clark Kent: Strength, laser eyes, enhanced senses

Q 15. Wonder Woman
A Diana Prince: Bulletproof bracelets, magic lasso

Quiz 4

Q 1. Which one of the disciples denied knowing Jesus three times?
A *Peter*

Q 2. Which is the correct order of creation according to Genesis?
A *Light; sky; earth and plants; heavenly lights; fish and birds; animals and humans*

Q 3. About how tall was Goliath?
A *Over 9 ft tall*

Q 4. What occupation did Ezra have?
A *Priest*

Q 5. What is Esau also known as?
A *Edom*

Q 6. Who was the oldest person in the Bible?
A *Methuselah*

Q 7. Write down the five books of Law
A *Genesis, Exodus, Leviticus, Numbers, Deuteronomy*

Q 8. Who was the first person to go to heaven who did not die in the flesh?
A *Enoch*

Q 9. Whose donkey talked?
A *Balaam's*

Q 10. Who was David's great-grandmother?
A *Ruth*

Q 11. Who led a rebellion against the authority of Moses and the ground swallowed them up?
A *Korah*

Q 12. What sign did God give to Hezekiah so he would know that God would add fifteen years to his life?
A *The shadow would go back ten steps*

Q   13. The punishment for raping a person is the same as murdering someone – death?

A   *True*

Q   14. Where was the 'school of Tyrannus' located?

A   *Ephesus*

Q   15. When Elijah built the altar on Mount Carmel how many stones did he use?

A   *Twelve*

Q   16. How many mighty men did David have?

A   *Thirty – he had three chiefs, but thirty mighty men*

Q   17. How old was Joseph when Pharaoh made him a ruler?

A   *Thirty*

Q   18. Who was hit on the head with a millstone?

A   *Abimelech*

Q   19. Who continued for two years in the school of Tyrannus, teaching the disciples and the people the Word of God?

A   *Paul*

Q   20. Who did Paul have a falling out with?

A   *Barnabas*

Quiz 5

Q 1. What was the approximate date that Moses wrote Genesis?
A *1446–06 BC*

Q 2. What are the Mari tablets?
A *Letters providing details of the customs language and customs of OT patriarchs.*

Q 3. Who was a preacher as well as a tentmaker?
A *Paul*

Q 4. Whose wife was turned into a pillar of salt?
A *Lot*

Q 5. What was the base construction of the ark of the covenant made?
A *Acacia wood*

Q 6. What is the Hebrew title of Numbers?
A *Bemidbar means 'in the desert'*

Q 7. What Israelite king built the Temple during OT times?
A *Solomon*

Q 8. What mountain did Moses climb when God promised him that he would see the Promised Land?
A *Mount Nebo*

Q 9. As Joshua and the children of Israel marched around the walls of Jericho the priests carried trumpets before the ark of the Lord. How many priests carried trumpets?
A *Seven priests*

Q 10. Who was Achon?
A *Josuah's son*

Q 11. How old was Joseph when Pharaoh made him a ruler?
A *Thirty*

Q 12. Who went with Moses to talk to Pharaoh?
A *Aaron*

Q 13. How old was Saul when he became king?
A   Thirty

Q 14. Which disciple walked on water?
A   Peter

Q 15. For how long did Jesus fast in the desert?
A   Forty days and forty nights

Q 16. Who had fasted in a similar fashion before Jesus?
A   Elijah

Q 17. What land was Jehoiakim from?
A   Judah

Q 18. Who wrote the book of Jude?
A   Jude

Q 19. What is another name for the Chaldeans?
A   Neo-Babylonians

Q 20. What was the tax collector's name referred to in Luke?
A   Zacchaeus

Quiz 6

Reinforcing Vision Statements or Values: Get your Vision Statement or Values. Access a free 'word-find' creator on the internet. Follow the steps to create a 'word-finder'.

Example: 'Jubilee Church is a community of God's people called to proclaim the words of Jesus and to practically demonstrate his love to a broken world in the power of the Holy Spirit.' (Paragraph 1 of Jubilee Church's Vision Statement). Get the people to say the vision back to you!

Example

```
V  P  E  T  T  O  X  O  T  S  N  E  K  O  R  B
R  T  E  T  D  E  M  O  N  S  T  R  A  T  E  I
F  F  L  E  Y  J  E  Y  Z  T  T  H  E  D  J  P
V  P  I  N  R  T  L  K  Y  Y  E  V  Z  P  N  N
N  O  B  S  X  E  I  Z  G  O  D  S  O  E  L  A
Y  W  U  K  U  F  C  N  C  N  D  N  U  O  P  T
T  E  J  X  Q  S  S  L  U  O  U  A  H  P  R  A
H  R  E  S  W  D  E  P  S  M  P  U  F  L  A  R
Q  M  U  L  E  W  R  J  C  I  M  T  X  E  C  W
P  N  D  L  Y  O  O  H  J  R  H  O  M  Y  T  S
F  O  L  D  C  A  U  R  L  S  L  T  C  G  I  N
O  A  F  L  C  R  N  O  L  O  D  I  U  T  C  O
C  M  A  F  C  X  T  O  I  D  S  R  E  C  A  M
M  I  Q  H  N  A  T  Q  S  D  U  I  O  T  L  U
M  F  E  Q  S  V  L  H  O  L  Y  P  W  W  L  W
F  U  L  O  V  E  J  K  G  Y  Z  S  K  X  Y  K
```

AND	BROKEN	CALLED
CHURCH	COMMUNITY	DEMONSTRATE
GODS	HIS	HOLY
IN	IS	JESUS
JUBILEE	LOVE	OF
PEOPLE	POWER	PRACTICALLY
PROCLAIM	SPIRIT	THE
TO	WORDS	WORLD

Events for the Masses

'If you build it, they will come.'
Field of Dreams

When working with groups of over twenty people, it can be easy for individuals to get lost in the crowd. The purpose of this chapter is to provide you with events rather than icebreakers. These can be run as part of the meeting, or can be the entire programme.

10 Tips for Mass Events

1 If you fail to prepare, you prepare to fail.

2 You don't have to do everything: Involve others by delegating responsibilities to them.

3 Advertise at least four weeks in advance to give guests enough notice.

4 The MC for the event needs to be well prepared. If the programme is led well, it will run smoothly.

5 Make sure that the team running the event is briefed in full before the event. Those who need programmes should receive them at least one or two days beforehand so they can familiarize themselves with what is planned.

6 If the event is run as an outreach, do not place pressure on visitors by shoving the gospel down their throat. Build relationship with them!

7 Create an atmosphere in the venue: Use lighting, music and décor creatively.

8 Welcome your first-time visitors publicly in order to make them feel at home.

9 Make sure that visitors are looked after for the entire time.

10 Spend time in prayer before the event!

Human Noughts and Crosses

✳ **9 chairs put into a block of three rows and three columns**

Set out nine chairs in a square three by three. Divide the group in two. One group should be designated 'the noughts' and the other group 'the crosses'. Everyone must be numbered. The groups should line up on the opposite sides of the square. You or another leader should shout three numbers (for example. 'three, eleven and sixteen') and all of those numbers from both groups must run to form a line by sitting on three chairs (using the same principle as when the game is played on paper). The first group to form a line gains a point for their group. There is, however, one rule. Each group *may not* form their line on the three chairs closest to them at any given time, and they *must* try to do so on the chairs furthest away from them! Once all of the numbers have been given a chance to go, the points can be added up and the winning group announced. This is a great game for after lunch to get the blood flowing from tummy to head again!

Mini Olympics

Divide the group into as many teams as you need. Aim to have one event per person; for example, if you have seven events, divide the group into teams of seven. This is where you have to get creative! The events do not have to be purely physical; you may have some mental challenges too. Do not tell the teams what the events are but let them find out as they go along. This way no team will have an advantage over another. Here are some ideas.

● **Event 1 – Ping-pong Ball Blow**
Set up a course in which the participants have to blow a ping-pong ball. The requirement is that they are on their hands and knees. The first one to reach the end of the course wins!

● **Event 2 – Cream Cracker Eating**
Give each participant four dry cream crackers; the first one to eat them all wins. This is tougher than it sounds.

● **Event 3 – Paper Plane**
Give each participant an A4 piece of paper. They have to construct a paper plane. The paper plane with the longest time in the air when thrown wins. (A crumpled ball of paper is not a paper plane for those who might try it!)

● **Event 4 – An Icebreaker of Your Choice**
This is where your creativity comes in. Use other icebreakers from this book or just make up your own!

Award points for first place through to last. The team with the most points wins!

Angels and Mortals

You will need:
* Paper
* Pens
* Hat

This is more of a long-term exercise than a one-off. It works best at a church or youth camp, or even at conferences or equipping weekends. Have every person write their name on a piece of paper. Put all the papers into a hat and pass it around the room with each person taking just one name from the hat. Everyone must keep the name that they have been given secret for the duration of their time together. The purpose of this exercise is to bless the person whose name you have daily, either by writing them a note, or buying them a small gift. Every night the notes/gifts are placed at the front of the room or meeting hall for the MC to hand them out. The person whose name you have is your 'mortal', and you are blessed by your 'angel'. Encourage the people to pray for their 'mortal'. At the end of the week/weekend, reveal to the group who their 'angels' were!

Ninety Seconds of Fame

This is a great event to plan in advance. Make sure that people have at least a week or two to prepare. In a similar way to a talent show, people or groups have ninety seconds to perform a drama, song or mime. Set up a judging panel to give feedback on each of the performances.

Around the World

You will need:

❋ Costumes, décor, information and interesting facts about a particular country
❋ Camera or camcorder
❋ Kitchen and dining facilities

Choose a country. The entire meeting will revolve around this country. Everyone can dress up in national custom. Cook a traditional meal from the country and decorate the room, house or hall where the event is being held according to the theme of the country (use flags, maps, pictures, ornaments and so on) – include table décor in this. Prepare some interesting facts about the country – these can be written on individual pieces of paper and wrapped up like little scrolls then placed at each table setting. Research the culture and some of the traditions. Find out the needs of the country and areas to be prayed into (this can usually be sourced on the internet).

Once everyone arrives, you can eat the meal together. This should be a fun time of fellowship. The outfits usually cause a lot of laughter, so don't forget to take photos (or bring a camcorder). After dinner, get each person to read out the interesting fact they have about the country. Share about the culture and traditions. Share about the needs. Pray together as a group for the country.

Tip: Divide the group into teams that can each take responsibility for the different elements of the evening (for example, food, décor, information and so on).

The Story

Get the group to tell a story. Each person must give one sentence, but the sentences need to begin with the sequential order of the alphabet. For example, 'A lady went to the market', 'There she saw a beautiful dress', 'She said, "I'll buy that", 'To her surprise, her friend also wanted to buy it'. And so on.

Food... Glorious Food!

Each person in the group should bring their favourite meal with them. They need to pay attention to the presentation! Each person will have an opportunity to show what they have brought and explain why it is their favourite thing to eat. Then eat all the food together... everyone having an opportunity to taste a little of everything.

Survey

You will need:

* Written questions
* Placards

First of all, prepare a list of questions that are similar to those used in a written survey and put the responses (for example, 'Very Poor', 'Poor', 'OK', 'Good', 'Excellent') on placards around the room. Now ask the questions and encourage the participants to move to the part of the room that best matches their response. Discuss with the group the reasons for their responses.

Rock 'n' Roll Evening

You will need:

* Fancy dress, music, food from the decade of your choice

Wear appropriate dress (Teddy Boy/full skirts with petticoats) and serve food from the fifties (or sixties, wearing the fashion of the day). Some ideas to go with the theme: A twist competition using Chubby Checker as your teacher, karaoke; 1960s music. If you choose to hold this event using another decade, why not try the seventies? Wear flares and tank tops, eat prawn cocktail/steak/Black Forest gateau and listen to Abba!

Ready-made Small Group Nights

*'Day by day continuing with one mind in the temple,
and breaking bread from house to house, they were taking their
meals together with gladness and sincerity of heart'.
Acts 2:46 (NASV)*

We have put together a series of small group guides. To run a successful meeting, make sure that you apply the tips given below. You must never underestimate how important preparation is. As the leader, it is vital that you know exactly where the meeting is going without having to rely on reading a programme.

10 Tips for Small Group Nights

1 If you fail to prepare, you prepare to fail.

2 Remember one thing: Atmosphere, atmosphere, atmosphere!

3 Be excited and real. People will catch it.

4 Make sure that visitors are your top priority; make them feel welcome and special.

5 Plan your small group nights months in advance; this takes huge amounts of planning pressure away from week-to-week running of the small group.

6 Use surprise! Keep people guessing all the time.

7 Hand out responsibility to members of the small group.

8 Try to avoid Christian lingo and jargon.

9 Continually share the vision of the small group.

10 Invite the visitors back from week to week.

BBQ Evening

This is a great one to invite non-Christians to. Simply spend the evening in fellowship over a BBQ and perhaps watch a movie afterwards.

A Night of Ready Steady Cook!

You will need:

∗ **Kitchen facilities**

The members can be divided into two groups and given a bag of ingredients. Tell them that their task is to prepare something simple and yet scrummy to bless the group, within a set amount of time. They will be 'filmed' and 'interviewed' as they cook. The other group will then need to sample their food and the reverse happens.

This is not only a great social evening for the small group, but is also great for inviting friends to. It can also be used as a team building exercise.

Pub Crawl!

This is a great way to get people out of their comfort zone and challenge any religious mindsets that they may have. The entire evening should be held in a bar over coffee. Worship can be a time of simply allowing each member to share what great things God has done in them over the week or month. Topics of discussion can be things such as 'Should Christians drink alcohol?' Ask questions such as 'What does it mean to be in this world but not of this world?' End the evening with each member sharing something they like or admire about someone else in the group. Make sure that each person gets a chance to be edified.

Gatecrash Another Small Group

This will need to be a top secret arrangement between the two group leaders. All the members of your group should meet in the usual place (your home, or the home of another member/leader). In shared cars (or on foot), make your way to the group that you are going to gatecrash. You can all gather around their front door and ring or knock. Spend an hour or so blessing them with goodies and then end by washing their feet and praying for them. You can return to your usual meeting place and spend some time in praise and worship, encouraging each other.

Night Prayer Walk in Town Among the Nightclubs

This is a great one for a Saturday night or even a week night if your area has nightclubs/pubs/bars. The aim is to go out in twos or threes and simply walk the area and pray, or ask the Father to bring divine appointments your way so that you can pray for and minister to people. This can be brought to a close by meeting up for a coffee. Share stories of the evening, and spend some time in fellowship.

Themed Evening: Religious Mentality versus Biblical Mindset

The religious mentality and the biblical mindset directly correlate with the Greek mentality and the Hebrew mindset. In order for this meeting to be most effective, encourage each member of your small group family to listen to session three of *The Glorious Church* series by Tony Fitzgerald in the week leading up to the meeting. This session is entitled 'Hebrew Mentality'.

This small group meeting will consist of creating an environment that fosters a discussion around the topic 'Religious Mentality versus Biblical Mindset'. What better setting for this discussion than a Hebrew dinner with your small group, hosted by you!

Before the Evening

Listen to session three of *The Glorious Church* series by Tony Fitzgerald.

Prepare Hebrew-style food such as matzos or flatbread equivalent, roast lamb, celery sticks, sweet peppers, lettuce, dates, nuts, honey and dried fruit. Make sure that you have red grape juice to take communion during your meal.

Organize some Hebrew music; in particular try to get hold of the Hebrew classic called *Hava Nagila*. You will be using it to organize a dance competition as an icebreaker before your meal together. Organize a prize for the winner(s).

Deck out your dining room/lounge with Hebrew-style decorations: Fabric and throws, green plants, woven baskets, candles and anything that would give the place a Mediterranean feel.

Encourage all of your small group members to come dressed appropriately for the evening.

On the Night

Start your evening with a dance competition using the song *Hava Nagila*.

During the meal, foster a discussion around the theme 'Religious Mentality versus Biblical Mindset'. At the end of your discussion, take a bit of time for communion.

Finish with worship and prayer.

Themed Evening: The Stages of Our Spiritual Growth

This small group evening is a travelling supper; each course will be hosted in different locations (either at different small group members' houses or in different rooms within a house) and will relate to one of the following stages of our physical growth:

● **Infant/baby:** For this stage serve soup; one of the key characteristics of babies is that they need fluids and milk.

● **Toddler:** For this stage serve greens; the key characteristic of the toddler season is the need for clear boundaries to contain the child's tantrums. A bit like discipline, greens are something people are generally not very keen on, but should have!

● **Teenager:** For this stage do not serve anything; instead, have a wild ice-breaker/activity prepared since one of the key characteristics of teenagers is that they always want to *do* something. For ideas on wild and fun stuff to do with your small group, browse through the 'Nowhere to Hide' section in this book.

● **Young Adult and Father:** For these stages serve meat; both of these stages are signs of maturity.

For each course, foster a discussion around the key characteristics of that stage and highlight the parallel with the spiritual equivalent. Encourage your small group members to back their suggested characteristics with appropriate Word-based examples. Discuss the differences between the last two stages, Young Adult and Father.

When you reach the final stage bring together all of the ideas discussed and get your group to think about 'where they are at' on the path of growth. Your small group members will be empowered to grow if they succeed in realizing and taking ownership of where they are truly at.

Themed Evening:
God's Heart for the Nations

For this small group evening, take your small group to the nearest airport. The evening will be held at the airport in order to focus members' thinking on the nations. Encourage everybody to bring a camera. Upon arrival at the airport, break the group up into teams of two to three people. Send each team on a timed run to ask as many nations-related questions to random people as they can in a set amount of time. For this, you will need to prepare a set of fun questions. For example:

● Where would you have to go to see the Great Wall?

● How many states are there in the USA?

● What is your idea of a great holiday: Beach bum or action hero?

● What is the capital of Bangladesh?

● How long did it take Phileas Fogg to go around the world in *Around the World in 80 Days*?

● What is the currency in Vietnam?

● In which city would you find the Sydney Opera House?

● In which country is Heathrow Airport found?

● Where are you flying to today?

Make sure that your small group members take plenty of pictures as they go on their run around the airport.

Have a prize ready for the winning team.

After that, choose a nice spot (for example, a coffee shop) where you can discuss the theme of your evening. Use the statement 'When God saved you, he had more than you on his mind.'

Themed Evening: Taking the Right Positioning Before Father God

This small group evening is aimed at offering each member an opportunity to assess the current state of their relationship with God. Are there any blockages, grey areas and other issues that affect their intimacy with the Father?

Serious Icebreaker: Personal Inventory

Take a moment and make an inventory of your own life. Bob Munger, in his little booklet *My heart – Christ's home* described the areas of one's life as the rooms of a house.

Consider the following areas of your life and their equivalent in room terms:

● Study. This room is your mind. Consider what you allow to go into and come out of it. It is the control room of the entire house.

● Dining room. Appetites, desires, those things on which your mind and spirit feed for nourishment.

● Bedroom. This is where you draw close to God and seek time with him daily, not just in times of distress and need.

● Tool shed. This room is where your gifts, talents and skills are put to work for God... by the power of the Holy Spirit.

● Lounge. The social area of your life; the things you do to amuse yourself and others.

● Cupboard under the stairs. The one secret place that no one knows about, but which is a real stumbling block in your walk in the Spirit.

Give yourself a grade in each room as follows:

A = excellent rating

B = good rating

C = passable, but needs a little dusting

D = barely pass, needs a lot of cleaning

Discussion Time

As a group, discuss the following statement: 'Elijah's provision in the desert came through ravens sent to the brook of Kerith. Had Elijah settled in a different location, he would have missed God's blessing in his life (1 Kings 17:1-5). As shown in Elijah's example, one's 'positioning' is a key to one's spiritual, emotional and material success in life.'

Worship and Ministry Time

Get your group to ponder upon the following question:

● Based on the discussion and the outcome of the personal inventory, what are the areas in which you need to properly position yourself to flourish in your relationship with God?

Go into a time of worship, giving each person the opportunity to repent and make themselves right with God in areas where they have not been properly positioned.

Note: To repent means to change one's mind for better, to heartily make amendments with an abhorrence of past sins (Strong's Greek Lexicon) – to turn from our sinful ways to God's better way. With regards to the theme of this evening, repentance is about taking the right positioning before God.

As the small group leader, be prepared to minister to people on specific areas as the Holy Spirit leads you.

Themed Evening:
What Do We Have to Give?

Icebreaker 1

Choose a fun icebreaker from the book.

Icebreaker 2

Each person must bring an item with them that reflects a facet of their character. Have a bag ready and ask each member to place their item in the bag as they arrive. The bag can be passed around the group. Each person should take one item out, and guess who it belongs to. Once you know who it belongs to, let the person explain why they brought it and what it says about them.

Edification

Discuss the question 'What do you have to give?' In doing so, consider the following:

● The enemy lies to us by saying 'You have nothing to give!'

We compare ourselves to others: Let's not covet another person's gifting or we will miss what God has for us and rob people of the blessing God wants to give them through us.

What the Word Says

Break up into groups and do a Word study on the different ways in which one can give. Let each group give feedback.

Practical Application

Challenge the members to each go and serve or be a blessing to someone this · week. Encourage them to be ready to give feedback next time.

Themed Evening: Perseverance

Icebreaker

Run a fun competition with a prize.

Edification

Read the following true story:

> In January 1956, pilot Nate Saint, along with fellow missionaries Jim Elliot, Roger Youderian, Pete Fleming and Ed McCully landed an MAF plane on a river sandbar and soon made contact with the isolated Auca people group. Days later, news emerged that they had all been speared to death. This tragic event profoundly affected future generations of this people group, now known as Waorani. It also greatly impacted the lives of Christians around the world.
>
> The former Archbishop of Canterbury, George Carey, remembers: 'I was just twenty years of age when news of the martyrdom of the Ecuador missionaries was released. I remember thinking that, for most of us, faith is so costless and so painless. Yet there in Ecuador, five young men with precious loved ones paid the ultimate sacrifice for Christ.
>
> The deaths of these five men opened the door to allow the love and forgiveness of Christ, as Nate's sister Rachel and Jim's wife Elizabeth returned in 1958 to live and serve among the Waorani. Later, so did Nate's son Steve, who has recently worked with Hollywood producers to release a major film about the event, *The End of the Spear*. The Waorani agreed to participate in the film to help others stop killing and live in peace.

Discussion Time
● How did the missionaries' families face the situation?
● Discuss the feelings and issues that they must have faced to 'run the race'.
● Look up a scripture passage on the theme 'endurance': 2 Timothy 2:3–4.
● Consider this: To endure is to outlast the problem.

Pray for one another

Themed Evening: Growing Outside of Our Walls

Beforehand

Ask the members of your small group to come dressed in the appropriate clothing to spend a bit of time outdoors during the evening. To foster a bit of anticipation, do not tell them why.

Prepare the routes that will be taken by the prayer-walking pairs on the night (see below).

Ask your worship leader to prepare songs that emphasize the strength of our mission to the community.

Prepare some fruit punch.

Welcome

Greet your small group with a glass of fruit punch as each person comes in.

Fun Icebreaker: Broken Telephone

You should whisper something into the first person's ear, and it must be whispered along the chain. The last person can speak it out aloud.

Note: Once the statement has been passed on to the next person it cannot be repeated. This makes the exercise even funnier!

At the end, the you can share what you originally started with.

Pass this statement along the chain (if you choose a different statement, make sure it is long):

● 'Don't tell anyone, but tonight the kingdom of God will advance as we break down strongholds and build righteously while we walk and pray; and Jesus is going to use you!'

Serious Icebreaker: 'Your Kingdom Come'

Ask the small group the following question:

● What did Jesus mean when he taught us to pray 'your kingdom come'?

Discuss how important it is that we may be part of the kingdom of God in our town/city and the nations.

Edification: Prayer Walk

Take your small group on a thirty to forty minute prayer walk around the neighbourhood where the small group meets.

Divide the group into pairs, and allocate the prayer-walking routes prepared beforehand to the different pairs.

Share some topics to be prayed through by each pair during their walk:

● God's kingdom to come to the neighbourhood

● People to hunger and thirst after righteousness

● Churches and church leaders around the area

● The level of the Holy Spirit to rise in the area

● The church to arise from slumber

● The salvation of the neighbours and specific people targeted

Allow some time to report back after the prayer walk.

Worship

Back at home, get your worship leader to lead you into worship.

Practical Application

Ask your small group members to continue to pray for the area during the coming week and allow a time of 'answer to prayer' feedback next time.

Themed Evening: Godly Order

Beforehand

Arrange with other members of the small group to bring and share pudding.

Welcome

Start the evening with shared pudding. Ask the small group members to serve one another and their leaders.

Fun Icebreaker: Pick-up Toothpicks

You will need:

* Enough toothpicks for the duration of the game

Drop all of the toothpicks in a bunch and take turns to go around and draw one out without disturbing the bundle. If you move another toothpick, you must miss a turn. The winner is the one with the most toothpicks at the end. If you draw out one successfully you can continue until one moves.

Use this icebreaker as an example for what comes later. We all have things in our lives which clutter them up. Learn how to draw some of them out without causing a major disturbance in your life.

Serious Icebreaker: What Does My Day Look Like?

Go around the group asking each person to list the responsibilities that he/she has in any one day, perhaps relating to their job, home, spouse, car or children. Be specific about the things that take up their time.

Edification: The Things That Hinder Me

Read out loud from Hebrews 12:1 and ask each person to ponder upon the following questions:

● What things hinder me or hold me back in my walk with the Lord?

● What would I name as the three things that most clutter up my life? Can I get rid of them or lessen their effect in a positive way? If not, which three things can I get rid of?

Get each individual to share their answers with the group and see if they can be divided into the following three categories:

● Spiritual

● Emotional

● Physical (for example, an untidy house)

Discuss this as a group.

Get each person to name a specific area in which they want God's help.

Get into pairs and pray for one another.

Worship

Consider having a time of thanksgiving without songs.

Themed Evening: Fruit of the Spirit - Love

Welcome

Welcome everyone with a hug and a special message, using an appropriate scripture saying that they are loved.

Fun Icebreaker: Guess the Picture

Prepare four pictures of things/personalities that people love, such as a puppy, a sports car, Mother Teresa or food. Cover each of the pictures with sixteen numbered squares of paper. Make sure that the pictures are not too easy to guess.

Split the group into teams. One member of the first team must choose a piece of paper numbered one to sixteen to be removed, and see if they can guess what the picture is. The next team has the next go. The winner is the first team to guess the picture. The game gets easier as the numbered squares are removed. Once the picture is guessed, go to the next one until all four pictures have been guessed.

Serious Icebreaker: Falling in Love

Get each person to share about the first time they fell in love. This doesn't have to be with a boyfriend/girlfriend, but can encompass things like pets or places.

Edification: Showing and Receiving Love

Use John 15:1–17 to show that love is rooted in obedience to God and has resulting actions.

In his book *The Five Love Languages*, Gary Chapman mentions that 'we must be willing to learn our spouse's primary love language if we are to be effective communicators of love.' This is not limited only to marriage but is true in every human relationship. The five love languages that he identifies are as follows: 1. Words of affirmation, 2. Quality time, 3. Receiving gifts, 4. Acts of service, 5. Physical touch. We each have a primary language through which we receive love. Based on this, discuss one another's love languages.

Pray into issues of:

● Fear of showing love

● Fear of stepping out and becoming vulnerable

● Fear of rejection

Worship: John 15:13

Use John 15:13 to focus on how God's love for us is rooted in the greatest action anyone could ever do.

Share communion together.

Note: During the Last Supper, communion was taken as part of the meal. It was not a specific ritual that Jesus and his disciples were following, but rather something that naturally flowed out of their time together. Therefore, when you share communion with your group, avoid being ritualistic about it.

Practical Application

As a group, plan a meal together at which each person can invite an unsaved friend.

Themed Evening: Fruit of the Spirit – Joy

Fun Icebreaker: What Makes You Happy?

You will need:

* CD player

Ask the members in your small group to bring a piece of music that makes them happy. Each person can play about two minutes of their track and share what it means to them.

Serious Icebreaker: Is Happiness Circumstantial?

You will need:

* *Cinderella* DVD/video
* DVD player/VCR

Show the clip of *Cinderella* when she wakes up in the tower and discuss the following statement and questions:

● A great majority of the European words for 'happy' stem from the word 'lucky'. Happy comes from a root word meaning 'chance' and 'fortune'. This implies that happiness is rooted in external things and circumstances that affect one's mood.

● Does the clip show joy or happiness? Which of the two is the deepest?

● How does sorrow prepare us and enlarge our capacity for joy?

Edification: Sources of Joy

Look at the following scriptures in reference to the sources of our joy:
- Faith: Romans 15:13, Philippians 1:25
- Hope: Romans 5:2, Romans 12:12
- Others: Romans 12:15
- God: Psalms 35:9 and 43:4, Isaiah 61:10, Luke 1:47, Romans 5:11, Philippians 3:1 and 4:4

Discuss the difference between worldly and godly joy.

Worship

Use instruments or CDs in your time of worship.

Give thanks to God for Christian joy and the joy that he brings to us.

Pray for one another.

Practical Application

Get each person to plan a way in which to bring joy to:
- Another small group member
- An unsaved person

Encourage everyone to come to the next meeting prepared to share who they brought joy to in the period leading up to the meeting, and how.

Themed Evening:
Fruit of the Spirit – Peace

Beforehand

For this evening, you will need to create a relaxed ambience by dimming the lights and using candles. Organize enough fresh flowers to give one to each person attending the evening.

Welcome and Icebreaker

Welcome everybody and get them to sit cross-legged on the floor, holding a flower.

Have tea and coffee together.

Arrange a painting or collage-making session on the theme of peace.

Hand out the circle of peace diagram and use it to discuss issues of peace and stress.

Edification: Godly Peace versus Worldly Peace

Discuss the following:

● John 14:27: 'Peace I leave with you; my peace ... I do not give to you as the world gives' (NIV). Based on this, what is the contrast between God's peace and worldly peace?

● Worldly peace is absence of conflicts, for example, sitting cross-legged with a flower in your hair!

● The peace that Jesus leaves is manifest within conflict.

● Could you say in the middle of conflict, 'It is well with my soul'?

Practical Application

Get everyone to give feedback on their attempts to bring joy to another member of the small group and to an unsaved person.

THE CIRCLE OF PEACE

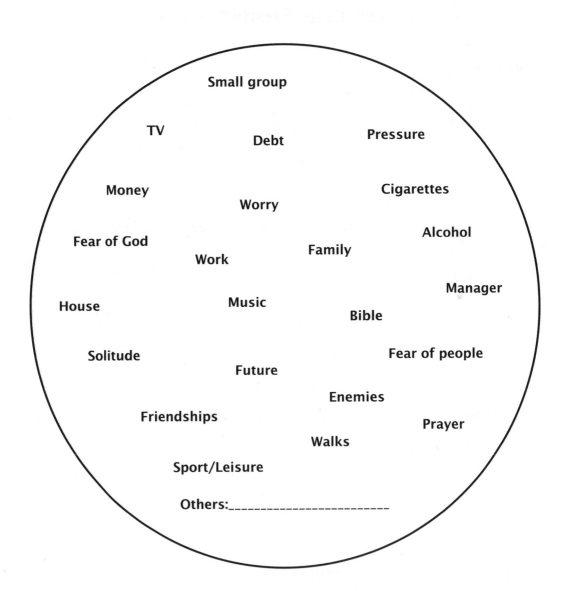

Small group

TV

Debt

Pressure

Money

Cigarettes

Worry

Fear of God

Alcohol

Family

Work

Manager

House

Music

Bible

Solitude

Fear of people

Future

Enemies

Friendships

Prayer

Walks

Sport/Leisure

Others:_____

The Circle of Peace

Put a ☹ by the peace-takers

Put a ☺ by the peace-givers

Themed Evening:
Fruit of the Spirit – Patience

Beforehand

Organize this fun icebreaker.

> ### You will need:
> * Cable ties (at least one per person)
> * Card decks (as many as you can organize)
> * Sugar cubes (a few boxes)
> * 2p coins (as many as you can organize)
> * A wobbly table
> * A prize for the winning team
> * Some gift-wrapping paper

At the beginning of the evening, you will present each person with a gift; a few cable ties per person. Make sure you wrap them in a creative and mystery-building way, like you would any decent birthday present!

Welcome

Give each person the nicely wrapped present with their name on it and tell them not to open it. Be excited and create anticipation amongst your group.
Have tea and coffee together.

Fun Icebreaker: Frustration Tournament

Ask each person to open their present.

Divide your group into three teams and tie the team members together using the cable ties.

Each team will compete in a tournament consisting of a series of frustrating team-building games and challenges:

● Build the tallest house of cards

● Build the tallest sugar-cube tower

● Make the most 2p coins balance on their side

All this needs to happen on the wobbly table! You can get each team to go through an activity one at a time and move on to the next challenge once all three teams have competed.

Keep a record of each team's score throughout the tournament. The winning team gets the prize!

Serious Icebreaker

Give an example of a time when you needed help to get through something. Share a time when you gave up trying. What was the consequence?

Edification: What We Need When Facing Trials

Romans 5:3–5: 'There's more to come: We continue to shout our praise even when we're hemmed in with troubles, because we know how troubles can develop passionate patience in us, and how that patience in turn forges the tempered steel of virtue, keeping us alert for whatever God will do next. In alert expectancy such as this, we're never left feeling shortchanged. Quite the contrary – we can't round up enough containers to hold everything God generously pours into our lives through the Holy Spirit!' (*The Message*)

Romans 5:3–5: 'And not only that, but we also glory in tribulations, knowing that tribulation produces perseverance; and perseverance, character; and character, hope. Now hope does not disappoint, because the love of God has been poured out in our hearts by the Holy Spirit who was given to us.' (NKJV)

Discuss the need for the following when facing trials:
● Encouragement of others
● God's order in our lives

Practical Application

Read Luke 11:5–9 and encourage your small group members with the promise of persevering in prayer. Encourage them to keep being patient and to keep on praying.

As a practical application, get them to pray for unsaved friends daily until your next meeting.

Themed Evening: Fruit of the Spirit – Kindness and Goodness

Beforehand

Organize some chocolates or little cakes to welcome your group members with.

Trust and ask God for a scripture for each person. Use a creative way to present it, such as writing it on a bookmark.

Welcome

Welcome your guests with the chocolates or cakes that you have organized beforehand, and hand out the scriptures as they arrive.
Have tea and coffee together.

Icebreaker

Ask and discuss the following question:
● Who is the kindest person you have met? Why?

Read out and discuss the following article:

'A newsman from New York went to see the work of Mother Teresa and to interview her. He asked her why she should expend her limited resources on people for whom there was no hope rather than attending people worthy of rehabilitation. Mother Teresa stared at him in silence absorbing the questions, trying to pierce through the façade to discern what kind of man would ask them. She had no answer that would make sense to him so she softly said: "These people have been treated all of their lives like dogs. Their greatest disease is a sense that they are unwanted. Don't they have the right to die like angels?"

Mother Teresa's calling was to enable those who died to do so beautifully. When asked how she could touch society's outcasts, she said: "I look into their eyes and in each one of their faces I see Jesus."'

Edification: Kindness

Kindness is not just a thought, but an action as well. Consider the following:

● **Kindness opens the human heart and makes way for the goodness of God.** The human heart was not created for harshness, rejection or pain; no one flourishes in such environment. However, people respond to kindness. Kindness breaks down barriers.

● **Kindness has the capacity to lead to salvation.** We can literally rescue people by a simple act of kindness and lead them to Jesus. When we show kindness, we proclaim Jesus' nature. It cuts across everything.

● **Kindness dignifies others.** Dignify means 'to invest with honour'. When we are kind to others, we declare that we care about their world. Kindness in this context has no lack of candidates; there are always many people around us who are hurting and crying out for somebody to care. Attached to our simplest acts of kindness is a powerful message of hope.

Practical Application

'All that is necessary for the triumph of evil is that good men do nothing' (Edmund Burke). Based on this, encourage the members of your group to identify the needs of those closest to you. As a small group, decide how you are going to respond to these needs. Pray for specific people who you are going to target with simple acts of kindness.

Themed Evening: Fruit of the Spirit – Self-Control

Beforehand

Contact the members of your small group and ask them to each bring £2 to the next meeting.

Welcome

Once everybody has arrived, take your small group out for an ice cream.

Icebreaker

Back at home, divide your group into gender-based groups.

Ask people to share about the following:
- When was the last time that you lost your temper and why?
- When did you feel pushed, but still exercized self-control in that situation?

Edification

A key scripture for this edification time is 2 Timothy 1:7.

The word 'self-control' takes its root from a Greek word meaning 'strength'. Self-control is a synonym of temperance. It is where we demand that the controlling power of our will come under the operation of the Spirit of God.

People lack self-control because they give their will free reign to do as it pleases rather than subjecting it to the Holy Spirit. Some areas in which we need to exercise self-control are anger, temper, eating and drinking habits (Proverbs 28:7), finances, lust and what we watch and listen to.

Without self-control in our lives we are rendered powerless: Have you ever tried to overcome something by your own willpower? It is usually not enough. It is only God's power and strength in us that enables us to command the controlling power of the will to subject itself to God's Spirit.

Galatians 5:25: 'If we live by the [Holy] Spirit, let us also walk by the Spirit. [If by the Spirit we have our life in God, let us go forward walking in line, our conduct controlled by the Spirit].' (Amplified Version)

What are the areas of your life in which you lack self-control? Eating habits? Drinking habits? Anger? Temper? Lust? Finance?

Take some time to pray for people.

Encourage each small group member to fast for one day during the week and pray about specific areas in which they need to apply self-control. Be aware that there might be some embarrassment or akwardness about sharing issues here; don't pressurize anyone to share anything they don't want to.

Practical Application

Ask people, 'What are the things that distract you from praying for unsaved friends?' Encourage each person to name a friend (or family member) that they are praying for, and to share any progress during the next few meetings.

Themed Evening:
Fruit of the Spirit –
Gentleness

Welcome and Fun Icebreaker

Welcome your people as they arrive.

Run a competition to find out who can hold a pillow in outstretched arms the longest. Make sure people's arms are parallel to the ground at all times!

Once everyone has had a go, ask the following question: 'What strengths were needed to do well in this task?'

Serious Icebreaker

Ask people the following questions:

● Who has ever attempted a task beyond their strength or ability?

● What happened?

Edification

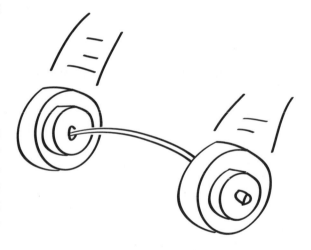

2 Corinthians 12:9: 'But he said to me, "My grace is sufficient for you, for my power is made perfect in weakness." Therefore I will boast all the more gladly about my weaknesses, so that Christ's power may rest on me.' (NIV)

'Gentleness' is better translated as 'meekness' or 'humility'. There is no adequate English word to describe the Greek root word that translates into gentleness in Galatians 5:23. This word conveys a meaning of strength, not weakness. To be meek means to have a mild and gentle temper, to be submissive. It does not mean to be weak!

We are called to display meekness:

● Firstly, before God. We should not fight with or against him, but rather accept his dealing with us as good.

● Secondly, with human beings. Even evil ones! God allows dealings with such people to purify and discipline us (Hebrews 12:1–7)!

The meekness manifested in Christ, which we need to reflect in our lives, is the fruit of power. The common assumption is that meek people are people who cannot help themselves; but Jesus was meek because he had the infinite resources of God at his command!

Worship

Around a communion meal, invite people to kneel and confess pride in their own lives. Encourage them to acknowledge their trust in Jesus Christ and the work he accomplished on the cross. Be careful not to pressurize anyone who feels uncomfortable about this activity.

Use Psalm 131 as a meditation to enter into God's throne room. End with a couple of songs.

Themed Evening: Fruit of the Spirit – Faithfulness

Welcome

You will need:

✳ **An ample supply of balloons**

As people arrive, give them each a balloon and ask them to blow it up and tie a knot.

Fun Icebreaker: Without Balloons, it is Impossible to Please...

Turn a table upside down and place it on top of about twelve balloons (make sure you aren't using a table you are afraid of damaging!). Ask your people how many of them they think the table will be able to support without bursting the balloons.

Add one person at a time and find out!

Serious Icebreaker

Ask and discuss the following: 'Which character from the Bible inspires you the most by their exercising of faith? Why?'

Edification

Read Jeremiah 1:11-12: 'The word of the LORD came to me: "What do you see, Jeremiah?" "I see the branch of an almond tree," I replied. The LORD said to me, "You have seen correctly, for I am watching to see that my word is fulfilled."' (NIV)

God asked Jeremiah what he saw. His answer pleased God, the almond tree being a sign of spring – new life and growth.

Based on this, challenge people concerning their sight: Can they see only the physical world and its immediate problems, or can they perceive the future that Jesus is leading them into?

Ask them what they are believing God for.

Hebrews 11:1 declares that 'faith is being sure of what we hope for and certain of what we do not see' (NIV). It is a 'conviction based on hearing' (see Romans 10:17). Therefore to have faith, we need to have heard God. The way to hear God is to read and know his Word.

Envisioning

What is the difference between faith and faithfulness in the context of sharing Jesus with our neighbours, family, friends and/or colleagues? In answering this question, invite people to ponder this statement: 'To be full of faith, one needs to be faithful'.

How can we use faith and faithfulness effectively?

Encourage people to pray specific prayers of faith for named people they are reaching out to.

Worship

Have a time of praise and worship based around giving thanks for God's faithfulness.

Teamwork

'Teamwork divides the task and multiplies the success.'
Author Unknown

10 Tips for Teamwork Activities

1 If you fail to prepare, you prepare to fail.

2 Communication is the key.

3 Observe the way that individuals react and respond.

4 See whether the teams appoint a leader or not. Leadership is always a factor of success.

5 Note how the team members speak to one another.

6 Note who does not get involved or remains at the periphery.

7 Make the groups as equal as you can in numbers, strengths and so on.

8 Bring variety in your use of different types of exercises: Use both physical and mental teamwork activities.

9 Encourage the teams to build their own ethos.

10 Have fun!

Sugar Cube Challenge

You will need:

✽ **3 boxes of sugar cubes per team**
✽ **A prize for the winning team**

Break the group into teams. The average size of each team should be four to five people. Supply each team with three boxes of sugar cubes. Say that the teams are to build a tower out of the sugar cubes. The highest tower will win the prize. If the tower falls before it is judged, too bad! Give them a time limit of thirty minutes.

The purpose of this challenge is to see how the team members interact with one another. There will be a variety of responses from the different members. Some will not partake at all; others will take charge and dominate their fellow team members. Some will make great suggestions but will not be heard; others will just criticize and not make any effort to encourage and build the team up. Each of these responses needs to be gently addressed in the group context after judging the work and handing out the prize. Avoid pointing people out, but comment on the various responses that you have seen. Encourage the group that, when it comes to teamwork, one may not have the expertise needed, but there is always something that can be done in support of what is going on!

It's a Wrap!

You will need:

✽ **Cling film**
✽ **Food objects**

This game is very similar to the 'Mummy Bake' icebreaker in the 'Nowhere to Hide' section of this book. Divide the group into teams of two and give each one a roll of cling film. One member of the pair must then be wrapped up in cling film by the other, as tightly and as safely as possible, avoiding the head. At the word 'GO!' the wrapped-up person must get to the floor and eat a food object off of a plate. Naturally the first person to finish is the winner. The same thing must then be repeated with the other teammate. Stage play-offs between the winners until you arrive at an ultimate winner.

Knock Knock... Who's There?

✳ A peg, egg or object similar in size for each team

Divide the group into two teams and give each of them an object. Set the challenge of going out as teams into the neighbourhood to knock on doors with a view to try and exchange this object for something of a bit more value. The teams have thirty to forty minutes. The team with the most valuable object at the end is the winner!

Let's Go Shopping!

✳ Ask everyone to bring a £1 coin with them, but do not tell them why

Get people into small teams and go to a supermarket. Upon arrival, set the teams a challenge to see how much each can buy for £1. This can be measured in weight, quantity or even size. You can set the challenge and make it only edible items. These items can then be used later as treats!

Island Paradise

Divide the group into teams of at least three. Say that the teams are about to be marooned on a desert island. Each team is able to take ten items with them. Give them fifteen minutes to discuss what they would take.. Each team must present to the rest of the group which items they would choose and why.

Blindfold Obstacle Course

You will need:

* **Set up an obstacle course beforehand**
* **Blindfolds**

Divide the group into teams of two and blindfold one person of each team. The other teammate must then lead their blindfolded team member around an obstacle course as safely as they can. This is great for anyone struggling with control or trust issues!

Chains Challenge

You will need:

* **A length of lightweight chain approximately five metres long for each team**
* **1 cable tie per person**
* **A digital camera for each team**

Break the group up into teams. The average size of each team should be four to five people. This activity should be run over the course of an entire day, for six to ten hours. Chain each team member together using the chain and the cable ties. Make sure that there is an equal distance between each team member. Once each of the teams has been chained, set them the task to take a picture of:

● The entire team in someone's car.

● The entire team holding a member of the public off of the ground.

These ideas are just to get you thinking, add another eight of your own that will make this exercise really challenging. Allocate approximately one hour for this part of the challenge.

Once this is done, get the teams to sit down together. Ask each member of the teams to share their testimony. Give each member thirty minutes for this; it will require approximately two to three hours for this part of the challenge.

Other challenges that can be done throughout the day:

● Give the teams various chores to do, such as dishwashing or cooking food for the other teams.

● Or you could have a training session on any topic you would like your group to brush up on. For this, make sure that everybody has notebooks, pens and Bibles if necessary. Remember that if one person leaves their stationery behind, the entire group has to go with that person to fetch it!

The purpose of this challenge is to break personal space. It is amazing how space-conscious we can really be. People will notice very suddenly just how much they tend think about themselves first rather than their team!

Newspaper Fashion Challenge

You will need:

* Scissors – 1 per team
* Sticky tape – 1 per team
* Tape measure – 1 per team
* Plenty of newspaper
* Black sacks – 1 per team
* CD player and music

This team building activity is broken up into two smaller challenges. The first challenge will enable the groups to earn their 'tools of the trade'. The second challenge is a 'fashion design' challenge.

Before starting, break the group up into teams of three to four people.

Challenge One: Earning the 'tools of the trade'

Before each team can take part in the 'fashion design' challenge, they will have to earn their 'tools of the trade': Scissors, sticky tape, tape measure, newspaper and a black sack. In order to earn their tools, each team must find the following items and trade them off against a tool:

● A round, flat stone the size of a 50p coin in exchange for the scissors

● Two paper clips in exchange for the sticky tape

● A used cinema ticket in exchange for the tape measure

● £3.72 in exchange for the newspaper

● A bird's feather measuring more than half an inch long in exchange for the black sack

Once a team has collected these items they will have forty-five to fifty minutes for the 'fashion design' challenge.

Challenge Two: 'Fashion design' challenge

Each team must prepare a full outfit of their own design (top and bottom) using the newspaper and sticky tape that they have just earned. The outfit to be designed will be tried on and modelled by a member of their team at the end of the allocated time. (If any team has not been able to earn all the tools, they will have to make do with what they *have* been able to get!)

To achieve this masterpiece, the time will be divided as follows:

● Time to design and plan the outfit over a cup of coffee or tea and a good chat: Fifteen minutes – Go wild!

● Time to take measurements of the model: Five minutes.

● Time to put your outfit together: Twenty-five minutes.

Encourage each team to use creativity and think outside of the box! They should not only design a garment, but also think about decorations and quirky features that will make it unique! The wilder, the better…

Then, the appointed models will be modelling their group's extravagant creations! Use the CDs you have brought to give each model some music for their walk. Get ready for some fun!

Build a Water Cannon

Supply your teams with raw materials such as bicycle tyre inner tubes, plastic containers, rope, water balloons and wood, and set the teams about twenty metres apart from each other. The object is to build a water cannon that fires, throws or shoots water balloons onto their opposition – the balloons can't be thrown with human hands! Set a time limit of twenty-five to thirty-five minutes. They can fire water balloons onto their opposing teams as soon as they get their cannons working! This can always end with a free-for-all water fight with leftover balloons!

Strategy and Teamwork with Water

You will need:

* String
* A pop-top water bottle
* Big buckets of water
* Dissolvable tablets

This game works best when played in a small area. Use the string to tie a tablet around each person's neck like a pendant or a necklace. Big tablets work the best. The object is to eliminate your opponents by squirting water at their tablets making them dissolve and disappear! When a tablet dissolves and falls out of the string, that person is out. People can refill their water bottles at the buckets.

Playdough Sculptures

You will need:

* Playdough
* Whistle

Break up the group into teams of four to five people, depending on the size of the group. Make sure each team has a large lump of playdough. Call out something that can be made out of clay. Do not make it too easy – for example, fire engine, skyscraper, jumbo jet and so on. One person in each team should begin to build the object. When you or another leader blows a whistle the next person in the team must continue to create the object. Blow the whistle at irregular intervals. When there is only one person left, each team must present their sculpture to the other teams.

Ultimate Team Member

You will need:

* A3 sheets of paper
* Marker pens
* Coloured pencils

Break up the group into teams of four to five people, depending on the size of the group. Give each team one A3 piece of paper and marker pen and some coloured pencils. The purpose of this game is for each team to draw the ultimate teammate. They are to sketch this teammate on the paper, and also list all the amazing attributes that they possess. Give the teams fifteen minutes to complete the exercise, after which they must present their 'Ultimate Teammate' to the other teams.

Director Madness

You will need:

* Digital cameras
* Transport
* List of objects

Break up the group into teams of no more than four. Make sure each team has a digital camera with video capabilities, and transport. Each team will be given the same objects to record on their camera. Create a list of objects then send the teams out to record them. Give the teams one hour to complete this task.

List of possible objects:

● A church steeple
● A zebra crossing
● A derelict building

These can be adapted to the time of year (for example, spring – a tree in blossom/daffoldils) or to where you live (for example, a war memorial/museum).

When the teams return watch all of the footage and check that they have the correct answers.

Lego Challenge

You will need:

* **A sculpture made of Lego**
* **Plenty of Lego blocks**

Before the meeting, design and make up your own Lego sculpture.

Break up the group into teams of no more than four. Say that they must make a sculpture out of their Lego blocks. Make sure that each team has the same blocks used in your sculpture, plus a few extra ones. Say that the purpose of this game is to recreate your original design but the challenge is that only one person may see the design, and they can only look at it for three one-minute sessions. When they return to their group after a one-minute session of study they may not touch the Lego blocks; the rest of the team must build on their instruction. If a team wishes to see the design a forth or fifth time, penalize them in points. At the end, judge the teams' efforts according to how close they are to the original.

This game is great to see how people communicate with one another, and also to watch if some team members just sit back and do not participate, or others dominate.

Crazy Stick

You will need:

* **A big pole**

This game is brilliant for getting people to work together, and it is almost impossible as well! Split the group into two lines facing each other. Get a pole the length of the line. Place the pole between the lines. Each team must hold it four to five feet above the ground by resting it on their index fingers. Then they should lower the pole to the ground as a team – but the pole must remain horizontal at all times, and everyone must be touching the pole at all times. Give it a go!

Egg Landing

* An egg per team
* A roll of toilet paper per team
* A metre of string per team
* A glue stick per team
* An orange per team
* A plastic bag per team
* An egg box per team

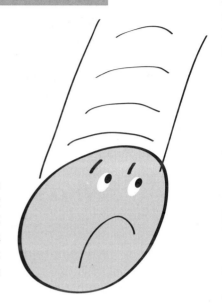

Break up the group into teams of no more than four. Supply each team with an egg, a roll of toilet paper, a metre of string, glue, an orange, a plastic bag and an egg box. The teams must try to build a structure that will support the egg if it falls. Think of it as an ejector seat from a fighter plane. The team whose egg survives the highest fall wins!

Blindfold Geometry

* A blindfold per person taking part
* Long ropes

Break up the group into teams of no more than six. Blindfold each member of the team. Give each team a long rope (over four metres). Call out various shapes like a square, pentagon, boat, car, vegetable; the teams must create these shapes on the floor with the rope whilst blindfolded. Teams can be awarded points on their accuracy.

Chair Football

You will need:

* Chairs
* Ball

Divide the group into two teams. Each person can sit on a chair somewhere on the field of play. They play a game of football but they may not climb off their chair. This is loads of fun. Use an oversize ball if possible and a soft ball for indoors.

Who's Who to You

You will need:

* A blindfold

This game is great for getting to know people's names. Arrange the team in a circle around one person who is blindfolded. The circle must walk around the person in the middle. When the person in the middle points at someone, the team must stop walking. The person who has been singled out should speak out loudly, 'Who's who to you?' The person in the middle must then try to guess their name.

IKEA Challenge

You will need:

✳ **Transport to the nearest IKEA store**

✳ **£2 per person taking part**

✳ **1 list of items per team (see below)**

✳ **1 camera per team**

✳ **Pens**

Divide your group into teams of six people. Say that each team has forty-five minutes to find the items on the list given to them. Organize a meeting point where all teams have to report at the end of the allocated time. Each team will be using a budget of £1 per person totalling £6. The remaining £6 per team will be used for hot dogs and ice creams at the end of the event. The search will take teams to the four corners of the shop. What is exciting is that certain IKEA names cover a range of items with varying prices. Teams will therefore need to pick the correct item of the range in order to spend their budget correctly. Whilst performing their search of the shop there are certain 'rules' that teams need to follow:

● Each team must stay together at all times.

● Team members must perform their search of the shop together and not break up. The reason for this is: It's more fun!

● Teams may not ask any shop assistant for help, or look in IKEA magazines to find clues about the item's type or location.

Upon finding each of the items of the list, each team need to take a picture of their members with the item found. Outrageous poses are welcome!

Teams should take plenty of crazy pictures whilst performing their search.

Once all items have been found, or at the end of the forty-five minutes allocated, teams must go and pay for their items and report to the meeting point.

The winning team is the one that has gathered all of the correct items in the quickest time.

When all teams have reported to the meeting point, go to the hot dog counter or store coffee shop to enjoy a treat together.

List of items to be found:

- HEJ (x 2)
- VIREN
- AKUT
- HURRA
- PLASTIS
- BONUS
- BILLIG
- DISKA

The Egg-mobile

You will need:

* A variety of clean rubbish such as bottles, news-paper, ice cream containers, margarine containers, paper, jars, toilet rolls

* Eggs

* Glue

* Sticky tape

* Scissors

* Paper

* Coloured pencils

Divide the group into teams. Set them the challenge to make a vehicle that will safely transport an egg down a hill or slope to the greatest distance without breaking! Give the teams twenty minutes to manufacture their vehicle and a further five to think about the name of it and how they would market and advertise it. Watch how they organize themselves and work together to produce a vehicle, give it a name and market its design with an advertisement to the other teams.

Island Hoppers

You will need:

* 3 sturdy chairs
* A 2 m plank of wood strong enough to stand on
* 2 poles
* A variety of other objects

Mark out a field of roughly 10 m x 10 m. All the objects should be placed on one side of the area, and the group must get all of them across to the opposite side without setting any part of their body on the ground inside the designated area! The chairs, the plank of wood and the poles are all special objects that can touch the ground within the area. Time the teams and analyze their work in order to give feedback after the event.

Teamwork Wins

You will need:

* 2 long ropes of at least twelve metres
* Water in a bucket
* Beacon to set an area boundary

Mark out a field of 5 m x 5 m. Divide the group into teams and set half of the people on one side of the field and the other half on the other side. The ropes must be on one side, and the bucket placed in the middle of the field. Say that no one is allowed into the field, and the teams must try to get the bucket out of the field without losing any water!

Tip: If you throw the ropes each side of the bucket and twist them together, the twist will tighten from both sides and you will be able to pick up the bucket and manoeuvre it out of the area.

Music and Lyrics

You will need:

✳ **3 quite famous songs and their backing tracks, for example *The Flintstones* theme tune, 'Summer Loving' from Grease and 'We are the Champions' by Queen.**

Give each team the task to come up with a unique musical based on the three songs, using their own words. Get team members to create characters and storyline. Each team must use a set length of each song, as set by you. For example: A minimum of a verse and chorus or a maximum of two verses and the chorus. Then they can act/perform for each other!